This Book is Presented to:

_____

From:

_____

Date:

_____

The NEW KIDS® Book of BIBLE FACTS

The New Kids Book of Bible Facts

Published by New Kids Media™ in association with Baker Book House Company, Grand Rapids, Michigan.

ISBN 0-8010-4441-3

Printed in the United States of America

1 2 3 4 5 6 7 — 06 05 04 03 02 01 00

The NEW KIDS Book of

BIBLE
FACTS

Anne Adams
Illustrated by Rick Incrocci

published in
association with

BAKER
A DIVISION OF
Baker Book House Co

For my kids
Michal and Alexandra Tyra

TABLE OF CONTENTS

GOVERNMENT

OCCUPATIONS

BIRTHS

(SEE NURSE, MIDWIFE)

The birth of a child was always a joyous occasion! While girls were treasured, every family hoped for at least one boy to receive the prized birthright.

Jewish women were ceremonially "unclean" after childbirth. They stayed in seclusion for forty days after a son's birth and eighty days after a daughter was born. A special sacrifice to purify them was made to the Lord. *(Lev. 12)*

Birthright

Every firstborn Jewish son received special privileges. These were part of his birthright:

- Twice the amount of his father's inheritance (Deut. 21:15-17)

- In early times, the privilege of priesthood (Exod. 13:1-2)

- Heir to his father's authority. (2 Chron. 21:3)

Bar meant "son" in Aramaic. In New Testament times, it was used before names to mean "son of." (Bar-Jonah meant "son of Jonah.")

Names

Names were carefully chosen. A name was not just a label. It revealed either a person's character, position, calling, or his relationship with God or other people.

Some Famous Bible Names and Meanings

Aaron - enlightened
Abram - father of height
Abraham - the father of a multitude
Adam - taken out of the red earth
David - beloved
Joseph - may God add
Joshua - Jehovah is salvation
Moses - taken out of the water
John - Jehovah has been gracious
Luke - light-giving
Noah - rest

Saul - demanded
Solomon - peace
Eve - life
Hagar - fugitive
Mary/Miriam - bitterness
Martha - mistress of the house
Naomi - my joy
Ruth - something worth seeing
Rebekah - captivating
Sarai - princess
Sarah - queen

Circumcision

When a Jewish boy was eight days old, the foreskin was cut from his penis. This was a sign that he belonged to God. *(Gen. 17:12)*

The procedure was usually done by the father, sometimes by the mother, and later by a Hebrew surgeon. *(Exod. 4:25)*

BIBLE BIRTH ANNOUNCEMENT

HERE YE! HERE YE!

Prince Solomon has arrived and taken up residence at the family palace in the City of David. He arrived in the year 991 BC of princely weight and height. Father King David and mother Bathsheba are doing fine.

BIRTHS (CONT.)

Feasts or banquets were often held on a birthday.
(Gen. 40:20)

Birthright Blunders

1. Esau, the firstborn son of Isaac, didn't care about his birthright when he was young. He sold it to his brother, Jacob, for a bowl of stew. Later, he realized the foolish mistake he had made. *(Gen. 25:29-34)*

2. Reuben was the firstborn son of Jacob, but his disobedience kept him from keeping his birthright. Instead it was transferred to his younger brother, Joseph. *(1 Chron. 5:1)*

Bible Nugget John 16:21 - John writes that a woman's pain and anguish while giving birth is quickly forgotten and replaced with joy when her child comes into the world!

WHAT FAMOUS PROPHET WAS KILLED ON HEROD'S BIRTHDAY?

John the Baptist. At Herod's birthday party, the daughter of Herodias danced for the king. Herod was so pleased, he promised to give her whatever she asked for. When the girl requested the head of John the Baptist served on a platter, Herod was greatly troubled, but he kept his promise. (Matt. 14:6-12)

MARRAIGES, WEDDINGS

Marriages were usually arranged by the parents. It was customary for a son's mother and father to choose his wife. If both families agreed with the arrangement, and if the son's family could pay the dowry (bride-price), a wedding took place.

The amount of the dowry depended upon what the bride was worth and how much the family could afford. Gold or silver was typical, but it could also be paid in jewelry, animals, goods, or service. (1 Sam. 18:22-25; Gen. 34:12)

Fifty shekels was the usual price for a new bride. A widow or divorced woman was worth only half that amount.

BETROTHAL
(Deut. 20:7)

- **The Promise**
  One year before a man and woman wed, they promised themselves to one another. This promise was similar to today's engagement.
- **The Contract**
  It was a binding, legal arrangement. The terms of the betrothal were in writing.
- **The Gift**
  Jewelry, usually semi-precious stones set in gold, was given to the bride-to-be and sometimes to her mother. The dowry could be paid at this time.

BIBLE WANT ADS

Father Seeking Daughter-in-Law

Abraham of Canaan seeking single, Jewish female **(SJF)** for son Isaac. Must be willing to move to the land of Canaan with Isaac and his family. If you love God with all your heart and believe in divine destiny, you may be the one. A generous dowry is offered. An angel, followed by my servant, will be in contact with you!

MARRIAGES, WEDDINGS (CONT.)

Girls were usually betrothed between 13 and 17 years of age. Their suitors were generally young men around 17 or 18 years old.

In Hebrew:

Kiddushin = Marriage or sanctification
Kallah = bride
Chatan = groom

Wedding Wear

- Kallah - Fine linen embroidered with gold thread. Her hair was often braided with jewels. The headdress was adorned with gemstones, gold ornaments, and later with gold and silver coins. Some wore a crown of flowers.

- Chatan - Fine linen, also woven with gold thread. Some wore a crown of flowers.

- Guest - Special clothes or wedding garments.

• The bride and groom wore crowns because in the tradition of King Solomon, they were proclaimed "king and queen" of the marriage festivities. *(Song of Sol. 3:11)*

• Wedding traditions varied. Sometimes, separate feasts were held for the bride and the groom. Some feasts lasted between seven and fourteen days, depending upon the wealth of the families.

Here Comes the Groom!

1. On the wedding day, the bride waited for her groom to arrive. Her attendants lit clay oil lamps so the house stayed bright as evening approached.

2. The bridegroom and his friends walked to the bride's home carrying torches.

3. Together, they led a joyful procession through the village with musicians playing drums and tambourines, torchbearers, dancers, family, and friends.

4. A feast was held at the bridegroom's house and the new couple was blessed by their parents.

• Most weddings took place in the fall when the full harvest was in. Entire villages were often invited. It was considered very rude to turn down an invitation to a wedding.

WHICH SON OF ISAAC AND REBEKAH WORKED 14 YEARS FOR HIS FUTURE FATHER-IN-LAW IN ORDER TO MARRY THE WOMAN HE LOVED?

Jacob! He worked seven years for Laban in exchange for the right to wed Rachel. On their wedding night, Laban switched his older daughter Leah for Rachel. One week later, Jacob married Rachel, too. He agreed to another seven years of service to pay off his dowry for his new wife! (Gen. 29:16-30)

Bible Nugget John 2:11 - While Jesus was attending a wedding at Cana in Galilee, the bridegroom ran out of wine for his guests. To save the groom embarrassment and to glorify God, Jesus changed the water in six stone jars into a fine and delicious wine!

BANQUETS, FEASTS

CONFUSED ABOUT ANCIENT ETIQUETTE? ASK DINAH!

Dinah's Tips for a Smashing Banquet

1. Don't forget! A banquet is expected at birthdays, marriages, funerals, sacrifices, at the laying of foundations, vintage (grape harvesting), sheep-shearing, and other special occasions.

2. Planning to invite most of the village? Issue a second invitation on the day of the banquet. Better yet, send your servant to personally escort guests to your home. You'll make a grand impression! (Luke 14:17)

3. Don't start your feast before the close of the day.

4. Greet guests with a kiss, then wash the dust from their feet. Anoint them with fragrant oil, and decorate their heads with garland. (Luke 7:45-46)

5. It's always a nice gesture to supply each person with a special robe to be worn during the festivities.

6. Seat your guests by rank or seniority. If entertaining during Old Testament times, guests will sit cross-legged on mats around low tables. New Testament timers are used to higher tables with chairs or couches!

7. A feast is not a feast without the wine. Be sure there's plenty to go around this time!

8. What to serve? You won't go wrong with lamb or kid stew with rice or barley.

9. Remember! Those with seniority always eat first. If you'd like to honor a special guest, serve him an extra portion, or fill his cup with wine until it runs over. (Gen. 43:34; Psalm 23:5)

10. Send a portion to a friend who could not attend. (Neh. 8:10)

11. Finally, liven it up a bit! Bring on the musicians, singers, and dancers. Anyone know a good riddle? (Luke 15:25; Judges 14:12)

Ask Dinah . . .

DEAR DINAH, I ALWAYS GET IN TROUBLE
WHEN I EAT WITH MY FINGERS. I TOLD MY
MOM I'M JUST PRACTICING AN ANCIENT
TRADITION. PLEASE HELP!
     -STICKY IN SAN FRANCISCO

Dear Sticky, Bright child! During banquets, utensils were
not commonly used. Two guests shared a bowl, and they
dipped their fingers in or used bread to scoop. Times have
changed, Sticky friend. It's time you did, too!

Dear Dinah, I am trying to teach my children
not to sneak their dinner food to the family
dog. They tell me you said it was part of some
old custom. What's all this about?
               -Fuming in Phoenix

Dear Fuming, Relax! I simply said that when guests were
finished eating, they wiped their hands on pieces of bread
before washing them with water. The bread was tossed on
the floor or thrown out the door to be eaten by the dogs.
Waste not, want not!

Dinah Says:

"Hospitality is key to a
successful banquet.
However, if any unruly, rude,
brazen, or otherwise
distasteful person shows up
at your party, throw 'em
out to the dogs!"

BANQUETS, FEASTS (CONT.)

When the rich hosted banquets, they spoke in Greek or Aramaic - never Hebrew. Food was served on platters of silver, bronze, exotic wood, or fine pottery. Goblets were beautiful blown glass. Entertainment was provided by musicians, poets, acrobats, and comedians!

→ Bible Nugget Luke 13:25 - The official host of a private banquet was the master of the house. When all of the guests had arrived, he shut the door of his home. Everyone knew what this meant. The festivities were about to begin!

SACRED FESTIVALS
My Yearly Sacred Planner
If found, please return to: Bar-Iri of Bethlehem

Month	Special Day	Notes
Nisan (April) 14	Feast of Passover	Most important. Celebrates God's rescue of Jews from Egypt. Eat unleavened bread, wine, bitter herbs, lamb. Retell Passover story. Thanks and praise to God! *(Lev. 23:5)*
15	Feast of Unleavened Bread	Celebrate with Passover Feast. All Jews, healthy and "clean" must attend above festivals. That means me! *(Lev. 23:6)*
21	Close of Passover	
Sivan (June) 6	Feast of Pentecost	Close of wheat harvest. Sing, dance, give thanks to God for crops and for giving law on Mount Sinai. Attendance required, Bar-Iri! *(Lev. 23:15-22)*
Tishri (Oct.) 1-2	Feast of Trumpets or Rosh Hashanah	Start of Hebrew New Year. Another day off! Blow horns and trumpets! Read God's law, feast. *(Lev. 23:23-25)* Forgive me, God, for sins of past year. I will fast and pray the new

SACRED FESTIVALS (CONT.)

10	Day of Atonement or Yom Kippur	year is a good one. Must attend. *(Lev. 23:26-27)*
15-21	Feast of Tabernacles	Family and I will live in tents to remember how forefathers lived in the wilderness. Offer many sacrifices. A week of great joy! *(Lev. 23:33-34)*
Kislev (Dec.) 25	Feast of Lights or Hanukkah	Celebrates rededication of temple to the Lord. Light the menorah for eight days!
Adar (March) 14	Feast of Purim	Remembers victory of Queen Esther and Mordecai over Haman of Persia. Give food gifts to friends, needy. Don't forget to read story of Esther.

Other Notes:
During one-day festivals, there is no work! During seven or eight-day festivals, there is no work on the first and last day!

The Year of Jubilee was celebrated every 50 years. Slaves were freed, debts were forgiven, and sold land was returned to its original owner. *(Lev. 25:8-17)*

In addition to the weekly Sabbath, the Israelites were "required" to take 19 yearly days of rest when the sacred festivals were observed. The festivals were celebrated as national holidays.

Trumpets were blown to announce the start of each festival. Most of the time, rams' horns were used, but sometimes special horns made of beaten silver were blown.

WHAT SUPERNATURAL OCCURRENCE HAPPENED EACH YEAR DURING THE THREE GREAT FEASTS?

God required EVERY male Israelite, physically able and ceremonially clean, to attend the Feasts of Passover, Pentecost, and Tabernacles. He promised to protect their homes and land while they were gone. Between the time of Moses and Christ, no enemy ever invaded the land during these three great festivals!

Bible Nugget Exod. 12:33-35;17-20 The Israelites were forced to leave Egypt so quickly, they left the yeast out of their dough so they wouldn't have to wait for it to rise. God told the Israelites to celebrate this occasion every year with the Feast of Unleavened Bread.

SABBATH

The fourth commandment God gave to the Israelites was, "Remember the Sabbath day by keeping it holy." This holiday began at sundown each Friday and ended at sundown on Saturday. It was a day of physical and spiritual renewal.

Sabbath Do's and Dont's

- DO use Friday afternoon to finish up your week's work. Women, do your cleaning, refill your lamps, prepare your meals in advance, do your laundry.

- DON'T do any kind of work on the Sabbath. This includes your slaves. Cooking, baking, beating with a hammer, lighting a fire, writing two letters, tying certain kinds of knots, or even helping injured persons, unless their lives are in danger, is NOT allowed. *(Exod. 35:1-3)*

- DON'T forget Friday evening prayer. Three sharp blasts of a ram's horn will signal the start of the Sabbath and prayer.

- DO have a special meal with your family after the service (prepared the night before). Recite the Kiddush - a special blessing said over the wine.

- DO attend a special service Saturday morning - more prayer and scripture readings.

IN HISTORY...... SABBATH SABOTAGE

168 BC
At the beginning of the Maccabean war, 1,000 Jewish soldiers were killed because they wouldn't defile the Sabbath by defending themselves in combat. Later, they decided that defensive action was acceptable. Offensive combat was still not allowed.

63 BC
In Pompey's efforts to take Jerusalem for Rome, he mounted massive battering rams against the city walls. Since Jews were not permitted to destroy siege works on the Sabbath, Pompey chose this day to use his battering rams to break in and take the city.

Trade was forbidden inside the city on the Sabbath so people weren't tempted to wheel and deal on this holy day. *(Neh. 13:15-22)*

A Sabbath Day's Journey was a distance of less than 2,000 paces or less than half-a-mile. This was the maximum distance Jews were allowed to travel on the Sabbath. Any farther was considered "work" and was not allowed. *(Acts 1:12)*

Those found guilty of working on the Sabbath were put to death. *(Num. 15:32-36)*

Sabbath Offering

On every Sabbath, priests offered two lambs in addition to a burnt offering. Frankincense and twelve loaves of unleavened bread, representing the twelve tribes of Israel, were also offered.
(Lev. 24:5-9)

Bible Nugget Matt. 12:1-14; John 5:1-18 - Jesus performed several healings on the Sabbath, much to the dismay of the Jews who considered it "work" and therefore unacceptable. He believed "the Son of Man is Lord of the Sabbath." On one particular holy day when he healed a paralyzed man, he said, "My Father is always at his work to this very day, and I, too, am working."

SACRIFICES, OFFERINGS

In ancient days, it was necessary for people to offer sacrifices to God. They did so in order to attain God's favor or forgiveness, to show their love, dedication and faith, or to simply give thanks.

LEVITICUS HANDBOOK 1-2-3
Moses' Guide to Sacrifices and Offerings

DO YOU. . .	OFFER . . .	AS A . . .
Want to show your devotion to God and be forgiven of general sins?	bullock, lamb, ram, goat, pigeon, or dove	burnt offering (Lev. 1)
Want to extend friendship to God or give thanks?	oxen, sheep, or goats	Fellowship or peace offering (Lev. 3)
Want God to forgive sins you committed by accident?	bullock, male or female goat, female lamb, dove, or pigeon	Sin offering (Lev. 4)
Want to be forgiven of your sins against God and others?	ram or male lamb	Guilt or trespass offering (Lev. 5)

Sacrifices were offered at every sacred festival on behalf of all of the Israelites. During the great festivals, the temple area was swarming with sacrificial animals for sale. Pigeons or doves were price. *(Lev. 5:7)*

MOSES' MAILBAG

Q. I'm a simple baker. I would like to offer a bull to God, but I just can't afford it. Will God be displeased with my goat?

A. Take heed man! You serve a merciful God.
Private offerings:
    (a) high priests - young bulls
        (b) kings - rams
           (c) middle class (merchants, landowners etc.) - goat or lamb
               (d) poor - pair of pigeons or doves

Rules To Remember

1. Every offering must be the property of the offeror. This means you cannot use your neighbor's sheep.

2. Every offering must be given with a sincere, humble heart and with deep reverence and respect. God cares more about your heart than the actual sacrifice.

3. Acceptable animal sacrifices are oxen, sheep, goats, and pigeons - free of sickness, injury, or blemish. Wild animals and fish are not acceptable to God.

4. Grain or meat offerings are wine, oil, or grain. You may use ears of grain, meal (coarsely ground seeds), dough, or cakes. *(Lev. 2)*

5. Sacrifices must be one of two kinds: animal (in which blood is shed) or bloodless, such as a vegetable.

SACRIFICES, OFFERINGS (CONT.)

DAILY TEMPLE SACRIFICES

Burnt offering: Lamb consumed completely in altar fire - every morning and evening.

Grain (also called meat) offering: Flour or cakes prepared with oil and frankincense - always follows the burnt offering.

Drink offering: Wine poured around the altar - presented with grain offering.

Public offerings were made in the tabernacle or temple on behalf of all Israelites. These included the burnt offerings made daily, on the Sabbath, and offerings made at sacred festivals. Private offerings were made any time by an Israelite and didn't have to be made in the temple.

In animal offerings, blood was sprinkled, splashed, poured, or smeared on the altar. Meat not burned was eaten by priests or sometimes the offeror. It was forbidden to eat the fat or drink the blood. *(Lev.1:11; 7:22-27)*

Some sacrifices were made by a priest, some with the help of a priest, and some without a priest. *(Gen. 15:9-10)*

The altar fire, in the tabernacle and later the temple, was never allowed to go out. Priests added firewood continuously to keep it burning. *(Lev. 6:8-13)*

HOLY INCENSE

- gum resin
- galbanum
- onycha
- pure frankincense

Blend equal amounts of the fragrant spices. Add salt, and grind into a powder. Offer it daily on the golden altar in the holy place, along with every grain offering, and on the Day of Atonement. *(Exod. 30:34-36)*

Bible Nugget Hebrews 10:5-10 - We are no longer required to make sacrifices because Jesus came to offer himself as the final sacrifice for us. His blood washed away all of our sins and made us pure and acceptable in the eyes of God. Now, in order to be forgiven, all we have to do is ask God!

DEATH, BURIAL

It was a very sad time when a loved one died. If possible, all work stopped for about a week. General mourning lasted for at least a month.

- Bodies were washed, rubbed with oil, and sprinkled with perfume, aloes, and spices. They were wrapped in long linen strips.

- Burials usually took place within eight hours. Jews thought it very shameful for a body to stay in the land of the living when the soul had already returned to God. . .

BIBLE OBITUARY

JESUS OF NAZARETH

Died, staked to a cross on Golgotha, in 30 AD He was born in Bethlehem around 5 BC to Mary and her husband Joseph. At 30, Jesus began his public ministry, preaching about God, his Heavenly Father. He performed miracles, loved the sinner, and taught the world that the kingdom of heaven is open to every man. Tombside visitation not possible. His garden tomb was found empty and his body missing! We are eternally grateful that through his death, resurrection, and ascension, he lives forever seated today at the right hand of his Father in Heaven! He is survived by his mother Mary, his brothers James and Jude, and all those whom he loved and touched.

DEATH, BURIAL (CONT.)

Expressions of Mourning

1. Mourners wore sackcloth made of black goats' hair, which they tore to express their grief. It was coarse and uncomfortable. Their discomfort wearing it expressed the discomfort of their grief. *(2 Sam. 1:2)*

2. Dust and ashes were sprinkled on the head. *(Josh. 7:6)*

3. The head and lower part of the face were sometimes covered with a veil. *(Jer. 14:3)*

4. In earlier times, their heads or beards were shaven.

5. Family and friends gathered around the body and wailed.

6. Professional mourners were hired by the family to help express public grief. *(Matt. 9:23)*

Bodies were carried through the town on biers or stretchers. Mourners, including family and friends, made a procession through the streets. Flutists often played.

Anyone who touched a dead body was ceremonially "unclean" for seven days. They had to be made clean in a special ceremony. *(Num. 19:11-13)*

The dead person's house was also "unclean" for seven days. No food was allowed to be prepared there during that time. Friends and neighbors brought over meals for the family.

After a period of time, bones were taken from their graves and placed in a stone box called an "ossuary."

GRAVES AND TOMBS

A. Graves for commoners were in open fields outside the city. They were usually on any side except the west since winds blew from that direction. *(Luke 7:12)*

B. There were private family cemeteries, but the poor were buried in common public graves. *(Gen. 47:29-30; Jer. 26:23)*

C. Hebrew graves were holes in the ground, natural caves, or tombs carved from rock. Tombs were often large enough for people to walk inside. *(Gen. 35:8)*

D. Tombs were sealed by boulders to keep out wild animals. Boulders were painted white to warn strangers to stay away. *(Matt. 23:27)*

E. Kings and prophets were buried within the city gates, in more elaborate tombs with several chambers.

Bible Nugget John 11:1-44 - When Lazarus died, he was buried in a tomb with a stone laid across the entrance. His friends and family were weeping and wailing. Even though Lazarus had been dead for four days, Jesus commanded him to "come out." Lazarus walked out of the tomb, still covered in his grave clothes!

FAMILY LIFE

Families could have many members living under one roof. There were husbands, wives, children, grandparents, and slaves. Later, married sons and their families often stayed in the home as well. Everyone had to pitch in and help!

JOB CHART

Earn a living by working a trade	men
Pay the bills	men
Collect the olives and dates	women
Grind the corn	women
Prepare the meals	women
Spin and weave the thread	women
Make the clothing	women
Take care of the animals	women
Fetch the water	women/children
Gather fuel	children
Teach sons a trade	dad
Teach sons laws and customs of Jewish religion	dad
Teach daughters how to manage a household	mom
Find suitable wives for sons	dad
Care for cattle/tend flocks	older children

The man was the spiritual and legal head of the household. A wife sometimes called her husband "lord" or "master."

TOYS

When all the chores were done, children played with friends and toys. They had whistles, rattles, and wheeled toys. The older children played hopscotch, jacks and board games like checkers, chess, ludo, and draughts.

Romans played a board game with dice. When the dice was rolled, each player moved a piece of wood around squares on the board. Their pieces were either robed, crowned, or given a scepter.

People in ancient times did not take very good care of their teeth. They did not use toothbrushes. Sometimes they ate anise to make their breath smell good.

WASHING UP

1.   When a guest enters your home, wash the dust from his feet. When you enter someone else's home, the host will wash your feet.
     (Gen. 18:4)

2.   Wash your hands before you eat.
     (Mark 7:3-4)

3.   Use public baths or pools to wash the rest of yourself. You may bathe at a river, if there is no bath. Don't forget to use soap! Rub yourself with herbs to smell nice.
     (Neh. 3:15)

FAMILY LIFE (CONT.)

"WHAT DID YOU SAY?"

Hebrew - the language of most Israelites who lived in Old Testament times. *(Isa. 19:18)*

Aramaic and Greek - spoken by most people in New Testament times, including the Romans. Diplomats and other important people in Old Testament times also spoke it. *(Dan. 2:4)*

Bible Nugget Mark 15:34 - When Jesus hung on the cross, he cried out in agony, "Eloi, Eloi, Lama, sabachthani?" In Aramaic, Jesus said, "My God, my God, why have you forsaken me?" Jesus spoke Aramaic and sometimes Greek. He could also speak and read Hebrew.

In very early times, a day was measured from sunset to sunset. The "heat of the day" was about 9 o'clock in the morning. The "cool of the day" was just before sunset. Many people went to bed with the sun. *(Lev. 23:32)*

HOMES

(SEE CARPENTER, TENTMAKER, STONECUTTER, MASON)

REAL ESTATE CLASSIFIED

TENT SALE

All kinds of tents for sale. The finest in animal skin, camel and goat hair. Small tents. Large family tents. Traveling with a horde? We have huge multi-room tents. Waterproof, sunproof, windproof. We've got one for you. The life of a nomad has never been easier. Contact Jesse, the tentmaker, for a great deal!

Tents were used by nomads who moved often in search of food and water for their animals. They were easy to take down and carry. Early Israelites, like Abraham, used them. So did desert dwellers like the Nabateans and the Bedouins. *(Gen. 13:18)*

Daily Living

House/Bethlehem

Courtyard doubles as kitchen and leads to cozy living room. Two sleeping chambers. Flat sunroof ideal for drying clothes, figs, grapes. Also good for sleeping, eating, praying. Two high windows keep house cool in summer, warm in winter. Wall hollows ideal for storing pots and making fires. Clay brick, whitewashed walls. Charming! Owner financing available. See Ira at town gates.

WHAT ABOUT THE FURNITURE?

- Furniture for most people was very simple:

- Beds were usually mats which were rolled up during the day. Sometimes people slept on raised platforms inside the house. Kings slept on bronze, iron, or exotic wooden beds.

- Chairs could be stools. Those who couldn't afford them, sat on mats or animal skins on the floor. Romans sat on dining couches with pillows when they ate.

- Tables in Old Testament times were low to the floor. Later, they were higher.

- Earthenware lamps burned oil.

- Lampstands were usually just niches in the wall.

In most homes, the animals stayed in part of the house. People slept and ate on the roof whenever possible. Doors were low, and adults had to stoop to enter. Most didn't have locks, but bolts or iron bars. *(Mark 2:4)*

Most homes were made of rough stone or mud and straw bricks. Tar was used for mortar. *(Gen. 11:3)*

Bible Nugget

2 Kings 4: 8-10 - When Elisha traveled to Shunem, he met a rich woman who invited him to stay for a meal. Whenever he was in town, he stopped by to eat. Since Elisha was a holy man, the woman was moved to make a room for him on her roof. She provided a bed, table, chair, and lamp.

FOOD, MEALS

There were usually two meals a day. Breakfast was light - bread, dried fruit, and cheese. It was usually eaten on the way to the fields or workplace. The main meal was eaten with the family at the end of the workday.

SUPPER MENU

(All meals served with your choice of leavened, unleavened, sweetened or unsweetened bread)

FISH - salted or dried with a hint of mint or dill.

CHICKEN - boiled or stewed with rice. Seasoned with a delicious blend of salt, onions, cumin, and garlic.

WILD FOWL (quail, dove) - boiled or stewed with rice in a rich gravy.

LAMB - stuffed in coosa (squash) or wrapped in tender cabbage or grape leaves.

SOUP - thick with peas, beans, and lentils.

PORRIDGE - made with fresh, ground corn.

FRUITS, NUTS, CHEESE - a tempting array of grapes, figs, olives, mulberries, pomegranates, apricots, plums, oranges, lemons, melons, dates, almonds, walnuts, and cheese curds.

EXTRAS - boiled or roasted locusts, fried grasshoppers, roasted corn.

DESSERT - dried figs boiled in grape molasses, honeycombs, honey donuts, locust biscuits, fig and cinnamon cakes.

BEVERAGES - water, red wine, honey wine, goat's milk, grape juice.

HOW TO MAKE BUTTER

Fill a skin bag with goat's milk. Hang it between three sticks. Shake it and squeeze it lots until it turns into butter.

Red meat was mostly served on special occasions. Pork, rabbit, and shellfish were unclean. They were not allowed to be eaten. *(Lev. 11)*

Egyptians ate their main meal at noon, rather than the end of the day. *(Gen. 43:16)*

Drinking water was sold on the street in goatskins.

Fruits and vegetables were bought fresh from the market as often as was needed.

Sack Lunches

Sack lunches were sometimes carried by workers. A typical lunch was two hollow loaves of bread filled with olives and cheese.

Bible Nugget

Gen. 25:34 - When Esau returned home from a day of hunting, he was very hungry. He smelled the delicious red lentil stew his brother Jacob made and asked for some. Jacob made Esau give him his valuable birthright in exchange for a simple bowl of stew.

CLOTHES, JEWELRY, HAIR

WHAT TO WEAR

Israelites wore clothing to express their relationship with God, or their feelings of joy or sadness. Clothing was usually white, purple, red, blue, yellow, and black. At festivals, bright colors were worn. At funerals, black, rough clothes were put on.

LADIES
1. Undergarment - long and tied with a bright sash.
2. Gown - long and fringed, sometimes with pointy sleeves
3. Jacket - small, tight-fitting, beautifully embroidered
4. Headdress - a plain shawl or a scarf set with pearls, silver, gold, or spangles.

GENTS
1. Undergarment - sometimes short like an undershirt, sometimes long.
2. Tunic coat - worn sometimes to the ankle.
3. Girdle - a cloth or leather sash worn around the tunic.
4. Cloak - large and loose, worn for warmth.
5. Headdress - cap (worn by the poor), turban, or headscarf

CLOTHES, JEWELRY, HAIR (CONT.)

Clothing was cotton, wool, or silk depending upon the wealth of the wearer.

The folds of a cloth girdle acted like a pocket to carry change, nuts, or other small things. A leather girdle (worn by soldiers, desert dwellers, or herdsmen) was supported by a shoulder strap and held a sword, dagger, and small objects.

WHICH PIECE OF CLOTHING WAS THE MOST IMPORTANT FOR A MAN?

His cloak. Sometimes it was called a mantle or robe. A cloak was used as a coat, a blanket, and even a saddlecloth. God said if you take a neighbor's cloak as a pledge, be sure to return it by sunset. It is the only covering he has for his body.

(Exod. 22:26-27)

Army generals usually wore scarlet robes. *(Judg. 8:26)*

A BIT ABOUT SHOES:

Shoes were usually made of soft leather. Sandals were a harder leather because they were made for rougher wear.

The soles of shoes were made of wood, cane, or palm-tree bark. They were attached to the leather with nails, and tied around the feet with "thongs." *(Gen. 14:23)*

Most travelers had at least two pairs of shoes.

WHAT WAS A COMMON WAY TO CONFIRM A BUSINESS DEAL IN ANCIENT TIMES?

One way was to pluck off your shoe and give it to the person you were in negotiations with! David went a step further. After making a covenant with Jonathan, he took off his robe, tunic, sword, bow, and belt and handed them over!
(Ruth 4:8; 1 Sam. 18:2-4)

JEWELRY

EARRINGS, NOSE RINGS OR NOSE JEWELS, SIGNET RINGS, TOE RINGS, ANKLETS, BRACELETS, NECKLACES. (ISA. 3:18; GEN. 24:22)

a. Men also wore earrings and rings.

b. Expensive jewelry was crafted from gold, silver, ivory, and precious jewels like red garnets and blue sapphires. Cheaper jewelry was made from bronze and glass.

c. Jewelry was taken as part of the war booty. It was also given in betrothal gifts. (Gen. 24:30)

d. High priests wore a breastpiece with precious stones. High officials wore gold chains. (Exod. 39; Gen. 41:42)

e. Camels often wore jeweled crescents.

CLOTHES, JEWELRY, HAIR (CONT.)

Makeup was used. Women painted their eyes, cheeks, and mouths. They also used a yellowish-orange paste on their fingernails and the palms of their hands. *(2 Kings 9:30)*

Do's and Don'ts of Hair Care

Women:

DON'T wear long hair loose in public.

DO braid it with flowers, ribbons, jewels.

DO use gold and ivory combs, gold hair pins and ribbons, gold hair nets, headbands, and jeweled tiaras, if you can afford it.

Men:

DO wear long hair and a beard if you are a Hebrew or Arab living in Old Testament times.

DO shave your beard if you are an Egyptian. (Gen. 41:14)

DO wear your hair short if you are a New Testament Jew.

DON'T ever clip the edges of your beard. (Lev. 19:27)

Bible Nugget 1 Peter 3:3 - Peter warns us that beauty does not come from outward adornments like braided hair, gold jewelry, and fine clothes. Rather, true beauty comes from a gentle, quiet spirit which is very valuable in the eyes of God!

SCHOOLS

(SEE SCRIBE, PROPHET)

In very early days, Israelites taught the children in their homes. They learned to read, write, and do basic math. They also learned by watching their parents and helping them. Formal schools were started after the Babylonian captivity.

LESSON OF THE DAY! "Class, we will begin by tracing the 22 letters of the Hebrew alphabet. Have your stylus and tablet ready!"

Sometimes, teachers held class outdoors beneath a shady tree. Students gathered at the teacher's feet to chant passages from the Torah or to have lively discussions.

SCHOOL DAYS, SCHOOL DAZE

Elementary school:	bet hasefer (house of the book)
Students:	boys 5 to 10 years old
Classroom:	the synagogue
School hours:	Sunday to Friday, daybreak to midday (about six hours each day)
Teacher:	the hazzan (official) of the synagogue
Desks:	wax-covered wooden tablets
Writing instrument:	stylus (pointy side to etch letters in wax, flat side to erase.)
Subjects:	reading, writing, math
Textbook:	the Torah - the only textbook ever used

SCHOOLS (CONT.)

The Torah

The Torah was the first five books of the Bible: Genesis, Exodus, Leviticus, Numbers, Deuteronomy. It was the written law composed of 613 different laws. It summed up all the Jews' beliefs. All education was centered around the Torah.

ADVANCED SCHOOLING

1. Bet talmud (house of learning)
   a. Boys 10 and up.
   b. Students delved deeper into the Torah. They analyzed it, discussed it, and chanted it aloud to help them memorize it.
   c. They were asked questions and taught to reason and argue intelligently.

2. Bet midrash (house of study)
   a. Young men 18 and up.
   b. Students studied to become a scholar - a teacher, rabbi, or scribe.
   c. Studies were more challenging: advanced Scripture studies, writing exercises for future scribes, astronomy, advanced math, natural science, geography.

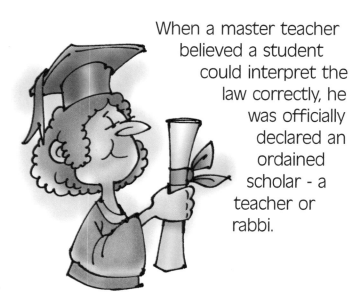

When a master teacher believed a student could interpret the law correctly, he was officially declared an ordained scholar - a teacher or rabbi.

MORE SCHOOL . . .

Scholars could further study with sages - great teachers who devoted their lives to meditation and teaching. They joined the sage during prayer, meals, and community service where they listened and learned as disciples. *(Ps. 119:99)*

Schools of the Prophets were formed to help train young men to be prophets. Disciples trained under respected leaders like Elijah and Elisha. *(2 Kings 2:3,5,7)*

WHICH APOSTLE WAS HIGHLY SCHOOLED IN THE JEWISH TRADITION, EDUCATED IN THE GREEK CULTURE, AND WAS ALSO A CRAFTSMAN?

Young Jewish men who wished to become doctors studied with priests who knew the art of ancient medicine.

Craftsmen (tentmakers, carpenters, etc.) usually learned their craft from their fathers.

It was Paul. He grew up in Tarsus, a city of Greek influence. Though he was a Jew, he was educated in Greek philosophy and learned to speak the language. He learned the art of tentmaking from his father, and was also trained under Gamaliel, the most honored rabbi of the first century! (Acts 22:3; Acts 18:1-30)

45

SCHOOLS (CONT.)

What About the Girls?

Girls didn't go to formal school. Their mothers taught them how to be good wives and mothers and how to care for a home, according to what was allowed in the Torah. They learned:

1. which animals were clean and unclean
2. how to prepare the food
3. to purify and set the table
4. to purify and decorate the home for the Sabbath and special holidays
5. the art of spinning and weaving
6. to treat illness with ancient remedies
7. to deliver babies
8. to sing and dance
9. to play an instrument like the flute, harp, psaltery, or tambourine

Bible Nugget

Matt. 28:19-20 - Jesus was similar to a sage. He devoted his life to teaching his disciples. He knew that one day they would be ready to share with the world the same message he had shared with them.

SYNAGOGUES

VISIT TO AN ANCIENT SYNAGOGUE

The synagogue was not like the temple. There were no priests there. Sacrifices were not offered. Jews might go to the synagogue for the following reasons:

a. to worship *(Acts 13:14-15)*
b. for school
c. to study and debate scripture
d. to hold court *(Luke 12:11)*
e. to gather - as in a community center or town hall *(Acts 9:2)*

"All groups must stay with your guide. No wandering through the synagogue!"

"Step up to the porch, please. Before worshipers entered the synagogue, they stood where you are standing now. They composed themselves before entering through one of three doors."

"Now inside, notice the many windows. The Torah was meant to be read in the full light. See the rows of benches on the sides? Men and boys over thirteen sat on one side. Women, girls, and young boys sat on the other side behind a screen. Only important members of society sat in the front row! All faced the speaker's platform."

"The Torah scrolls were stored in an ark. This ark sat in a cubbyhole in the side wall which faced Jerusalem. The scrolls were covered in fine linen and brought out after the opening blessings and praises. A member of the congregation was chosen to read the scripture. Any questions? Exit quietly to your left. NEXT GROUP, PLEASE!"

SYNAGOGUES (CONT.)

Before every synagogue service, the floor was rubbed with water and mint.

The Torah was read aloud every Sabbath, festival, and new moon. It was also read on Mondays and Thursdays (market days). Certain scripture readings could be read by anyone, even children.

Most towns with ten or more Jewish families had a synagogue.

URGENT NEWS BULLETIN!

Synagogues throughout Palestine and the surrounding regions have invited the apostle Paul to preach a Christian message to their orthodox Jewish congregation! This is possible, sources say, due to the "FREEDOM OF THE SYNAGOGUE POLICY." This policy allows guest rabbis to teach a sermon of their choosing. Is it possible Jewish scholars underestimated Paul? Rumor has it the message of Christ is spreading like wildfire...

Bible Nugget

Matt. 4:23 - Jesus was so well educated in the Jewish tradition, he was called a rabbi. He spent much of his ministry teaching the gospel in the very synagogues he sat in as a boy chanting the Torah.

TABERNACLE

Q. What was the tabernacle, anyway?

A. It was God's home on earth. When Moses received the Ten Commandments on Mount Sinai, God told him to build a Holy Sanctuary where he could dwell and sacrifices could be offered. *(Exod. 25:8-9)*

Q. How was it made?

A. It looked like a large tent and was built from materials given by the Jews: gold, silver, and bronze; blue, purple, and scarlet fabric; fine linen; goat skins and hair; ram skins; acacia wood; lamp oil; spices and incense; onyx and other gems. *(Exod. 25:1-7)*

Q. But they were traveling through the wilderness. Did they just leave it after they built it?

A. No. The tabernacle was portable, like a tent. They took it down and set it back up each time they made camp. *(Num. 9: 15-23)*

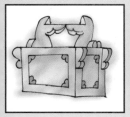

Q. Last question! What was the ark of the covenant?

A. The ark of the covenant was a wooden box covered with gold. Inside were the two tablets of the Ten Commandments, a gold jar of manna, and Aaron's rod. It was kept in the Holy of Holies where God dwelled, the most sacred place in the tabernacle. *(Exod. 16:34; 1 Kings 8:9)*

Bible Nugget

Exod. 40:34-38 - When the tabernacle was built, God dwelled in his home on earth! The glory of the Lord filled the sanctuary with a cloud. At night, fire was in the cloud. The Israelites broke camp and traveled only when God's glory left the tabernacle and the cloud lifted.

TEMPLES

The temple replaced the tabernacle as the first permanent Holy Sanctuary. It sat high on Mount Moriah in Jerusalem and was the chief place of worship and sacrifice.

The Tale of Three Temples

(Chapter One) King Solomon's Temple

When David was king, he was distressed that God's house was only a tent. "Shouldn't the Lord, our heavenly king, dwell in a temple grander than earthly palaces?" he wondered. While God whispered in his ear, he drew up the blueprints. Sadly, David was not allowed to build it. The honor fell upon his own son, Solomon, the next king of Israel.

In 950 BC, Solomon imported the finest materials from around the world and used only expert craftsmen to build the first holy temple. It dripped with gold and held a sea lined in copper and 10,000 gallons of water! God dwelled in his new home, and people came to worship and offer sacrifices and praise. Nearly 400 years later, it was destroyed by the Babylonians. Jerusalem was burned, and many Jews were forced to live in exile in Babylon. The temple had been silenced. *(2 Sam. 7:1-4)*

(Chapter Two)
The Restoration Temple

In 538 BC, a few Jews were allowed to return to Jerusalem. They were poor, but determined to rebuild their temple. Occasionally, they begged their friends, still in Babylon, to send more money. Sometimes, the old men looked at their work-in-progress and remembered the grandeur of Solomon's Temple. They wept in despair, "What kind of a house of God is this?" The young men, born in exile, had never seen the other temple. They rejoiced, "It is magnificent! It is a place of our own to worship God!"

When the rest of the Jews returned, they joined in the work and the temple was completed in 515 BC. Through the years, they tried to make it more beautiful. Didn't they know God didn't care? He had a home on earth once again. Music and singing filled the temple halls. *(Hag.1-2; Ezra 3:12)*

TEMPLES (CONT.)

(The Final Chapter) King Herod's Temple

King Herod had a reputation for making magnificent buildings. It was hard not to notice the modest temple sitting high atop Mount Moriah. Every time he looked at it, he felt itchy. "Perhaps the Jews won't mind if I replace a few things, here and there," he murmured.

Forty-six years later, the once modest temple was white marble. Plates of gold reflected the rays of the rising sun. Jesus worshipped in the last temple, and the glory of God filled the sanctuary like never before. When he was crucified, his glory left. The final temple was burned by the Romans in AD 70 and was never rebuilt. After the resurrection of Christ, the temple was no longer necessary. God's glory dwelt in his believers. *(John 2:20)*

• Today, all that remains of Herod's temple is a portion of the Western Wall called the "Wailing Wall." It is the most sacred of all Jewish religious sites. The name refers to the sounds of sadness made by Jews who visit the holy place. They offer prayers, written on pieces of paper and placed in chinks in the wall.

Did You Know?

When Herod rebuilt the temple, he tried to please the Jews by hiring 1,000 priests trained as masons and carpenters. The priests worked in the most holy areas of the temple which would otherwise be defiled by non-priestly hands. Eighty years later, much of their inexperienced work fell apart and had to be redone!

Bible Nugget Acts 21:27-29 - Once, when Paul was at the temple, he was seized by Jews and arrested. He was accused of bringing Greeks into the temple. Any non-Jews found in the inner temple were put to death. Paul had been accused wrongly, but he was later sent to Rome to be tried.

SPREADING THE GOSPEL

Jesus trained twelve disciples to spread the gospel - the good news of his life, death, and resurrection. He knew they wouldn't understand it all until after he was gone. What he told them, and what they told the world, was brand new!

JESUS "MAKES WAVES" BY DINING WITH SINNERS

Jesus of Nazareth, commonly referred to as "Jesus, the son of God," was seen today having dinner at the home of Matthew, a known tax collector. Other tax collectors were reportedly present.

When questioned as to why he ate with men of ill repute, Jesus replied, "It is not the healthy who need a doctor, but the sick...I have not come to call the righteous, but sinners."

This comes not long after sources say Jesus actually

The Fab Twelve

Peter, **Andrew**, James (son of Zebedee), **John**, Philip, **Bartholomew**, Thomas, **Matthew**, James (son of Alphaeus), **Simon the Zealot**, Thaddeus, **Judas Iscarot**, Matthias (replaced Judas after he killed himself)

healed a paralyzed man and calmed a storm by speaking to the wind and the waves.

An anonymous source reveals that Jesus, accompanied by his twelve disciples, is drawing huge crowds by teaching a message of love, forgiveness, redemption, and hope. *(Matt. 8:23-27; 9:1-12)*

WHY DID JESUS OFTEN CLASH WITH THE PHARISEES?

The Pharisees were a very powerful, religious group who believed that each of the 613 laws of the Torah must be strictly observed. They would rather let someone die on the Sabbath than break one of their laws to help them. It was the Pharisees who criticized Jesus for eating with the tax collectors. Jesus said their rules were like burdens.

(Acts 15:5-11)

SPREADING THE GOSPEL (CONT.)

Gospels → first books of the New Testament, **Matthew, Mark, Luke, John** reveal:

1. The Life of Christ - teaches about God's character and how we should strive to be like him.

2. The Death of Christ - teaches that through the sacrifice of Jesus, we are washed clean of our sins and made pure in the eyes of God.

3. The Resurrection of Christ - teaches that we have eternal life through Jesus.

• Paul helped spread the gospel more than any other person. He wrote 13 New Testament books, traveled on three different missionary journeys, helped start and support many churches, and brought the message of Christ to the Gentiles (non-Jews).

Bible Nugget Matt: 3:11, 12 - John the Baptist helped prepare the way for the ministry of Jesus. He baptized people in the Jordan River as a sign that God was washing them of their sins. But he told them one will come who will "baptize you with the Holy Spirit and with fire."

THE OLD GOVERNMENT

(SEE JUDGES, ELDERS)

The Israelites had a very long history dating back to the time of Abraham. As their numbers grew and the years passed, their form of government often changed to meet the needs of the people.

Ancient Rulers

1. God

When Moses led the Israelites out of Egypt, God was their ruler for 40 years in the wilderness. Moses received instructions and laws directly from God and passed them on to the people. *(Exod. 19:5-8)*

2. Elders

A group of elders was chosen to represent the people during the wilderness journey. Later, they ruled communities and had the authority to make major decisions. *(Ruth 4:1-4)*

3. Judges

The Israelites settled in Canaan and were ruled by judges for several hundred years. They led during peacetime

THE OLD GOVERNMENT (CONT.)

and were also leaders in war. Some famous ones were Deborah, Gideon, and Samson. *(Judges 2:18)*

4. Kings
The Israelites decided they wanted a king, like other countries had. Saul became the first. There were good kings like David and his son Solomon. There were also bad kings like Jeroboam. *(1 Sam. 8:5)*

5. Conquering Countries
The kingdom of Israel was often conquered by foreign armies. When the Syrians controlled Israel, they allowed the Jewish high priest to rule the land. He was, however, always subject to Syria.

6. Cities of Refuge

God told Moses to make sure "cities of refuge" were scattered evenly throughout the Promised Land. If someone committed a crime by accident, they were legally allowed to hide in these cities until they were given a fair trial. *(Josh. 20).*

Bible Nugget 1 Kings 4:7 - King Solomon divided the kingdom into twelve districts and appointed a governor to each one. Each governor was in charge of supplying provisions for the king and royal household for one month of the year.

THE NEW GOVERNMENT

here was endless fighting in Palestine. In 63 BC, the
Roman government decided the only way to bring
peace to the land was to occupy it.

(SEE TAX COLLECTOR)

Roman Rule

King Herod the Great - He ruled most of Palestine. Though he
was half-Jewish, the Jews hated him. He rebuilt the temple, but
he also ordered all infant boys in Bethlehem put to death in an
attempt to kill baby Jesus *(Matt. 2:1-18)*.

Herod's Sons - Herod died, and the country was divided into
three areas. They were ruled by Herod's three sons: Archelaus
(Judea and Samaria), Herod Antipas (Galilee), Philip (Iturea). *(Matt.
2:19-23)*

*When Judea was made a Roman province, a Roman governor
(procurator) was put in charge. Pontius Pilate ruled during the
days of Jesus. *(Matt. 27:1, 2)*

THUMBS UP!

1. Roman rule brought peace to a region plagued by civil war. The order lasted about five centuries.

2. Romans knew the wisest way to govern Palestine was to give the Jews some space. They tried to be tolerant of their customs and religious practices.

3. The Roman army built paved roads which made travel easier. Their presence also did away with many of the bandits which threatened travelers. This allowed trade to flourish and the gospel to be spread throughout much of the ancient world.

THUMBS DOWN!

1. As the emperor became more powerful, Romans began to worship him as a god. They tried to make the Israelites say "Caesar is Lord."

2. When Christians refused to worship Caesar, they were persecuted. Many were thrown to the lions.

Bible Nugget Luke 6:15 - One of Jesus' disciples was called Simon the Zealot. Zealots were a group of people who hated Roman rule so much, they tried to overthrow the government by using violence.

THE SANHEDRIN

The Sanhedrin was the highest Jewish court of justice which ruled in Jerusalem. They tried serious crimes, especially crimes against God.

Who's Who

The Members
Of the 70, there were elders, former high priests, and scribes. Many were Pharisees.

The President
He was the high priest, sometimes called the "prince."

65

SANHEDRIN (CONT.)

The Meeting Place
The council met in the temple complex on any day except the Sabbath and holy days.

The Quorum
At least 23 members were needed to conduct business.

A Majority
A bare majority could acquit. A majority of two was necessary to condemn. If all 70 members were present, a majority of one could acquit or condemn.

The Judgment
Fast judgments were frowned upon if someone's life was at stake. If a person was condemned to death, the punishment was not carried out until the next day.

The Herald

As the condemned was led to execution, a herald walked ahead and cried out:

"Paul has been found worthy of death. If anyone knows anything to clear him, let him come forward and declare it."

When the Sanhedrin ruled during the days of Jesus, the death penalty could not be carried out unless it was first approved by the Roman governor. This is why Jesus was brought before Pontius Pilate. *(John 18: 28-32)*

In Old Testament times, judges or elders tried cases outside the city gates.

67

WHICH MEMBERS OF THE SANHEDRIN WERE SECRET DISCIPLES OF JESUS?

Nicodemus (a leading Pharisee) and Joseph of Arimathea. Nicodemus went to see Jesus secretly in the night and learned about the kingdom of heaven. Both men prepared Jesus' body for burial and laid it in a new tomb belonging to Joseph. *(John 20:38-42)*

Bible Nugget Acts 6:8-15; 7 - Stephen was a man of great faith. His teachings about Jesus angered so many Jews, they falsely accused him of crimes against God. He was taken before the Sanhedrin. When Stephen proclaimed his beliefs before the council, they dragged him out of the city and stoned him to death unlawfully.

CRIMES AND PUNISHMENT

Crimes and their punishments were listed in the Torah. All criminals had to be punished according to the Law. If they weren't, those who handed out the justice would be guilty of breaking the law, too.

CRIMES PUNISHABLE BY DEATH

1. murder
2. hitting or cursing a parent
3. blasphemy (saying bad things about God)
4. working on the Sabbath
5. witchcraft
6. adultery
7. kidnapping
8. worshipping idols

CRIMES AND PUNISHMENT (CONT.)

Some Forms of Execution

1. stoning - common for blasphemy *(Deut. 22:24)*
2. burning *(Lev. 20:14)*
3. the sword *(Exod. 32:27)*

Hanging was not a form of execution. Bodies were hung on trees after the people were dead, to bring more shame. They had to be buried by nightfall so the land would not be spoiled *(2 Sam: 21:60)*.

Crucifixion was introduced by the Romans. Jews thought it was the most horrible form of death.

Less Serious Crimes and Punishment

1. If a man steals a sheep - he must pay back four sheep. *(Exod. 22:10)*

2. If a man's bull injures another bull, and it dies - they must sell the live bull, then split the money and the meat of the dead bull equally. *(Exod. 21:35-36)*

71

CRIMES AND PUNISHMENT (CONT.)

OTHER PUNISHMENTS

1. Hard labor *(2 Sam. 12:31)*
2. Flogging *(Deut. 25:2)*
3. Throwing people from cliffs
   (Luke 4:29)
4. Stocks *(Jer. 20:2,3)*

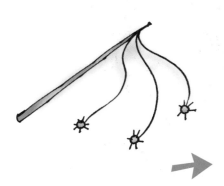

Criminals were flogged with a three-pronged whip while laying on the ground or tied to a pillar. They were only allowed by law to receive forty lashes. If they received more, the person who did the flogging was punished. *(Deut. 25:23)*

Cisterns were underground wells for storing water. Empty ones were sometimes used as prisons. *(Jer. 38:6)*

DEATH OF A BELIEVER

"The following men are found guilty of spreading the gospel of Jesus Christ. They are accused of sharing the truth that the kingdom of heaven is open to Gentiles, of bringing sinners to task, loving the unlovable, forgiving the unforgivable. They are a threat to citizens of the great Roman Empire and are hereby sentenced to death....."

1. PAUL - beheaded under the direction of the Roman Emperor Nero.

2. PETER - crucified by the Roman Emperor Nero. He did not feel himself worthy to die in the same manner as Jesus, so he asked to be crucified upside down.

3. ANDREW - crucified in Achaia (Greece) on an X-shaped cross.

4. JAMES (son of Zebedee) - "put to death with the sword" by Herod Agrippa I.

5. STEPHEN - stoned to death by members of the Sanhedrin.

6. JOHN THE BAPTIST - beheaded under Herod's rule.

Bible Nugget Acts 16:22-24 - When Paul was on his second missionary journey, he and Silas were dragged before authorities and accused of crimes against the Romans. They were stripped, flogged (beaten) and thrown into prison. Their feet were placed in stocks (wooden frames with holes) so they could not escape.

BAKER

Baking bread was an important task carried out mostly by women or slaves. Wheat made the most tasty and nutritious bread, but those who couldn't afford it used barley.

In the earliest days, grain was pounded with a stone mortar and pestle. *(Prov.27:22)* Coarse bits, not yet flour, wer used to make the dough.

Later, a hand mill *(Exod. 11:5)* was used to produce flour. Grain was ground between two rough millstones. A rotary mill was used even later.

Bread was baked fresh every few days, since it quickly turned stale or moldy.

Sweet Treats

- Cakes were sweetened with honey or flavored with mint or cinnamon.

- Honey doughnuts were cut into animal shapes and deep fried in olive oil.

- Locust biscuits were made with ground, sun-dried locusts, honey, and wheat flour.

RECIPE

RECIPE FOR ANCIENT BREAD

1 grind coarse grain or flour, preferably wheat or barley water

2 salt a little fermented dough saved from the previous day

3 mix the above ingredients.

4 knead the mixture in a wooden bowl or kneading trough to form a pliable dough. It will be sticky.

5 let the dough rise for several hours.

6 shape into flat loaves and bake.

In more modern times, cities and larger villages had a public baker. Women prepared the dough, then brought it to town to be baked in larger public ovens. The baker's boy returned the bread to its owners, carrying some of the loaves on his head.

Public bakers were so important in Jerusalem, an entire road was called "Baker's Street." *(Jer. 37:21)*

Royal bakers made breads or cakes just for the royal household. *(Gen. 40:5)*

BAKER (CONT.)

OVENS

Bowl Oven. The simplest and one of the most ancient. It was made of clay and had a removable lid. The bowl was inverted on small stones. Hot, dry dung was heaped over it.

Jar Oven. Large stone or copper jars were half filled with hot pebbles, heated wood or grass. When the jar was hot, the top was closed and the dough was placed on top to bake.

Pit Oven. This clay oven was built partly below ground and partly above. The fire was made inside.

Barrel Oven. These were especially popular in Palestine and Syria. A barrel shaped hole in the ground was plastered with clay and heated with dung and straw.

Bible Nugget Genesis 18:6 - Sarah baked bread for the three visitors, probably by placing the dough on the hot ground which had been heated by a fire. It was then covered with embers!

BARBER

Public barbers worked on the open street, but rich families employed their own personal barbers.

A BARBER'S KIT:

→ **razor**
→ **scissors**
→ **basin**
→ **mirror**

HEBREW TIMES

BARBER (CONT.)

WHO NEEDS A TRIM? →

Gentiles and Modern Jews. They usually shaved their beards, unlike ancient Jews who were not even allowed to clip the edges. Many kept their hair very short. *(Lev. 19:27; 1 Cor. 11:14)*

Nazirites. Their hair was long and uncut, but sometimes they shaved it off as part of their vow. *(Numbers 6:18)*

Hebrews. Shaved their heads while in mourning, or to show humility and repentance. *(Job 1:20)*

The Inflicted: The Jews inflicted with infectious skin diseases, like leprosy, were required to shave all their hair, even their eyebrows, in order to be considered clean again. *(Lev. 14:8-9)*

Egyptians. Kept their heads and beards shaved unless they were in mourning. *(Gen. 41:14)*

Bible Nugget
Ezekiel 5:1 - God told Ezekiel to take a sharp sword and use it as a barber's razor to shave his head and beard. He was to divide the hair into three parts to show God's people the fate of Israel.

BEGGAR

During Old Testament times, the law of Moses provided for the poor. There was not such a need for people to beg for food:

"When you reap the harvest of your land, do not reap to the very edges of your field or gather the gleanings of your harvest. Do not go over your vineyard a second time or pick up the grapes that have fallen. Leave them for the poor and the alien." Lev.19:9-10

Later, when cities grew, begging became very common. Many beggars lived off of other people's money or food. People looked down upon them.

How to Beg

Run your forefinger across your teeth and hold it up. This means you are poor and hungry.

Bible Nugget

Luke 16:20 - Lazarus was a godly beggar who couldn't work because he was sick. He sat by the gate of a very rich man. Day after day, the rich man refused to feed him. When both men died, Lazarus was carried to heaven, but the rich man suffered in hell because of his selfishness.

CARPENTER

Carpentry was an important trade. At least one carpenter could be found in most large villages or cities. Most carpenters were like Joseph. They earned a simple living making things like roofs, window shutters, plows, and yokes. They also made furniture including tables, chairs, and storage boxes.

Nazareth was known as a town of carpenters. They often displayed their trade by wearing a wood chip tucked behind one ear.

Royal Carpenters

King Hiram of Tyre sent David the most skilled Phoenician carpenters to help build his royal palace. *(2 Sam. 5:11)*

Solomon used the finest carpenters to build the temple. *(Ezra 3:7)*

Josiah employed them to help repair the broken temple. *(2 Kings 22:5-6)*

Herod used them to shape doors and window frames from great logs for use in his temple.

CARPENTER (CONT.)

→ **Ancient Egyptian Toolbox**

ax - to chop wood
adze - to shape the wood
saw - to cut wood to precise sizes
square - to lay out right angles
awl - to put small holes in wood or leather
plumb line - to make sure a wall was perpendicular
hammer / glue-pot

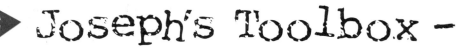

→ **Joseph's Toolbox -**

Centuries later, Joseph would have added these tools:

bow drill and bits - to drill holes in wood
stone-headed hammer - to drive nails
wooden mallet - to hammer wood pieces together
iron chisels/files - to shape and carve
ruler and compass - to measure
wood plane - to smooth or shape
spoke shave - to cut thin slices
supply of nails

- The most common wood used in Palestine was the soft Jerusalem sycamore, the hard olive wood, and oak.

- Imported cedar from Lebanon was very expensive. It was used in the palaces and temples of David, Solomon, and Herod.

- Algumwood from India was also used in Solomon's temple. It was black on the outside, ruby red on the inside, and smelled sweet.

- Iron tools, which were very hard, were used for working stone. The much softer bronze was often used in woodworking.

Bible Nugget Mark 6:3 - When Jesus was preaching in his hometown of Nazareth, the people were amazed by his wisdom and the miracles he performed. They had a hard time believing that Jesus, the son of a carpenter, could really be the son of God.

CHAMBERLAIN

(ALSO CALLED STEWARD, GOVERNOR, AND CHIEF MINISTER)

A chamberlain was a personal attendant to the king or other royalty. He watched over the palace and made sure all business was conducted according to royal custom.

Later, the role of the chamberlain grew more important. He had the high honor of introducing the king . . .

"Hear Ye! Hear Ye! His Royal Majesty, King of all Judea and Samaria ... Herod Agrippa!"

Bible Nugget Acts 12:20 - Blastus was the chamberlain of King Herod Agrippa, but he was not as loyal as the king would have liked. The people of Tyre and Sidon bribed him in order to secure an audience with the king!

CLERK

(ALSO CALLED RECORDER)

Originally, the clerk was a servant who cleaned and decorated the temple. In later years, his role grew to one of huge importance and authority.

BIBLE WANT ADS:

Looking for trustworthy man of high esteem. Must be able to keep and organize all public and government records, oversee all treaties, and occasionally prepare drafts of royal wills for the scribes. Will also be responsible for bringing all complaints or requests from the king's subjects directly before the king. Apply in person at royal palace.

The city clerk or city recorder was often the mayor of the city or a high official of the kingdom.

Bible Nugget

Acts 19:35 - While Paul was preaching in the city of Ephesus against the worship of false gods, a huge riot broke out. The people dragged Paul's helpers away. The city clerk quieted the crowd, dismissed the people, and brought order back to the city.

CUPBEARER

(ALSO CALLED BUTLER)

The Bible Badge of Courage Award is hereby presented to the CUPBEARER for his unflinching bravery in executing his duties as follows:

➤ risking his life by tasting all food and wine before serving them to the king - just in case they are poisoned.

acting as the king's trusted confidant by listening to all of his stories and keeping all of his secrets.

Bible Nugget Nehemiah 1:11 -

Nehemiah was a captive Jew in Persia, but he was so well thought of by King Artaxerxes, he was chosen to be his royal cupbearer!

DOCTOR

(ALSO CALLED PHYSICIAN)

In the earliest days, priests were expected to act as doctors and help the sick. Later on, Jewish men studied medicine under the guidance of priests. Many of their methods were passed on.

The Israelites also learned a lot about medicine from the Egyptians, whose physicians were very advanced for their time.

Common skin diseases included: leprosy, syphilis, smallpox, boils, and scabies.

Other common diseases were: tuberculosis, typhoid fever, malaria, and dysentery.

Treatments

For most skin diseases	mineral baths; ointments and pastes made of herbs and oils
Boils	a hot fig paste, such as the one applied to King Hezekiah by Isaiah. (2 Kings 20:7)
Wounds	salt to clean and disinfect olive oil and wine (Luke 10:34) honey
Snake bites/ scorpion stings	balm resin
Stomach ailments	wine (1 Tim. 5:23)
Other internal diseases	medicines made from roots, pounded into powder, and leaves and berries boiled in water
Toothache	garlic
Sore gums	yeast rubbed on the infected area

PRESCRIPTION FOR SEASONAL DISORDER:

dried carob beans, fresh dates, aster oil, honey, water

Mix the ingredients well and drink every four hours. Patient will experience severe sweating which will rid the body of poisons.

Early prescriptions were often written on clay tablets.

DOCTOR (CONT.)

4 Common Surgeries –

performed in New Testament times

1. **Removal of arrowheads**
2. **Amputations**
3. **Cataract removal**
2. **Tracheotomies**

Some Roman Medicinal Tools:

speculum
cup for bleeding
box of medicines
hook - for removing tissue
scalpel
spoon - to warm salves
probes
forked instrument - to remove
arrowheads

THE MOST FAMOUS PHYSICIAN IN THE BIBLE?

The evangelist Luke. He was thought to be Paul's personal doctor. He was so loved, he was called "beloved physician." (Col. 4:14)

Bible Nugget Mark 25:23 - While Jesus was on the cross, soldiers offered him a drink of wine mixed with myrrh. This mixture was commonly used as a painkiller. Jesus did not accept it.

DYER

Town dyers used large vats to dye thread and cloth. They could be found plying their trade in busy marketplaces of cities or villages.

A dyer wore a brightly dyed piece of cloth somewhere on his body so people would know his trade.

Dyes

Deep red or crimson -
Came from female worms or grubs.
Used to dye the robes and shoes of the rich, the dress of a warriior.

Blue -
Came from the pomegranate rind.
Needed for the ribbon and fringe of the Hebrew dress, the lace of the high priest's breastplate.

Purple -
Came from the Murex shellfish. It was the most costly dye.
Only the wealthy, like kings, wore robes or clothes of this color.

After 1200 BC, Canaanites were called Phoenicians.

Do you know why?

The Canaanites became famous for the red dye they produced. The Greek word for red is

"phoinos!"

Purple dye was called "Tyrian purple" because it was made by the Phoenicians in the city of Tyre. Making it was such a stinky process, the city often smelled like garlic and people avoided going there!

Bible Nugget Exodus 25:4-5 - When God gave Moses directions for building and decorating the tabernacle, he called for offerings of blue, purple, and scarlet yarn as well as ram skins dyed red.

FARMER

(ALSO CALLED PHYSICIAN)

THE ANCIENT FARMER'S ALMANAC

Planting time in Palestine? Consult your calendar:

Sept. - Oct. (Tishri): Sirocco desert winds are gone. Cooler west sea winds carry in early rains and soften the ground. Good time to ready the soil and plow!

Oct. - Nov. (Heshvan): Sow your barley and wheat seeds first, followed by rye, millet, flax, and vegetables.

Nov. - Dec. (Kislev): Winter months are unpredictable. Keep an eye on those stalks.

Dec. - Jan. (Tebeth): Here come the winter rains!

Jan. - Feb. (Shebat): First blooms on trees should appear now. Be sure to sow the summer grain before the end of Shebat.

Feb. - March (Adar): Almonds are in bloom. Time to pick the citrus fruit.

March - April (Nisan): Barley harvest begins. Pray for late rains. Watch for hot east winds with the coming of the dry season as well as occasional hail storms.

April - May (Iyyar): Barley harvest! Guard against palmerworm, cankerworm, caterpillar, and locust which will kill your crops.

May - June (Sivan): Wheat harvest is here! Crows, sparrows, and fungus are your enemies. Vintage season begins.

June - July (Tammuz): Grapes, figs, and olives ripen under the hot summer sun. Tend to your vines.

July - Aug. (Ab): Don't despair of hostile heat and growing bulrushes.

Aug. - Sept. (Elul): Gather in the fruits and vegetables, in particular the grapes, figs, and olives.

FARMER (CONT.)

In Almanac History

Today marks the anniversary of the beginning of farming, one of the oldest occupations in the world. Our honorees: Adam and Eve in the first garden called Eden. *(Gen. 2:8)*

Almanac Advice

Pay your tithes! Egyptians, pay a portion of each crop to your landowner, the king. Hebrews, pay your tithes to God who owns your land. Offerings of seed, grain, and freshly baked bread are customary. *(Lev. 2)*

COMMON FARMING TERMS:

sickle - a tool used to cut grain. First made of flint, then metal.

threshing - separates the grain from the stalks. The stalks are beaten with a rod or trampled under the feet of oxen.

threshing floor - the place where grain is threshed, usually clay soil packed hard and smooth.

winnowing - separates the valuable seeds of grain from the light, useless chaff. Piles of threshed grain are scooped up with a winnowing fork and tossed into the air. The grain falls close, the lighter straw farther. The lightest chaff blows away in the breeze.

The land in Palestine was so rich, there was no need to fertilize. Every seventh year, however, farms, olive orchards, and vineyards were required to lie in fallow, or rest.

When Egypt fell under Roman rule in 30 BC, Egyptian farmers produced most of the grain needed to feed people in the entire Roman empire!

Bible Nugget Ecclesiastes 3:1 - Solomon, in his infinite wisdom, tells us, "There is a time for everything, and a season for every activity under heaven: a time to be born and a time to die, a time to plant, and time to uproot."

FISHERMAN

Fishermen spent most of their time on the Sea of Galilee, a large, freshwater lake. Since fish was a large part of the diet, the role of the fisherman was very important. Fish were salted, pickled, dried, and sold or traded to other countries.

Fishing Report

Fishing action remains excellent on the Sea of Galilee. An abundance of fish, up to thirty-seven kinds, can be found in these waters on any given day. Tilapia galilea and sardines abound. Herring and salmon are a sure bet with the dragnet. The barbel, blenny, and eel-like silurus continue to be taken, as well.

LAKE CONDITIONS

The lake elevation of the Sea of Galilee is 685 feet below sea level. It is 13 miles long, 8 miles wide, and up to 150 feet deep in parts. Fresh water inflows from the Jordan River are constant.

Fishermen's Advisory! Lake is highly unpredictable! Calm conditions are typical most mornings, but late afternoons can bring sudden, violent storms with 20 foot swells. Use extreme caution.

RECORD FISH

Species: Tilapia galilea, also called St. Peter's fish
Record: Fish was caught with a silver coin
  in his mouth! (Matt. 17:27)
Year Caught: about 30 AD
Fisherman: the disciple Peter
Location: Sea of Galilee

➡ Night fishing was common. Fishermen dragged a torch above the water to attract the fish to the surface. They began at dusk and returned at sunrise with their catch.

FISHING NETS

1. Drag-net: Very heavy; required several men to work it. Net was let down from the side of the fishing boat, and floats marked its location in the water. Later, it was drawn to the shore or into the boat.

2. Hand-net or casting net: A small, circular net thrown from the shore or shallow water.

3. Bag-net: Used to trap fish in deep water.

Bible Nugget Luke 5:1-7 - Simon Peter, James, and John returned from a night of fishing with empty nets. When Jesus told them to cast their nets again into the deep water of the Sea of Galilee, they were doubtful, but they obeyed him. When they returned, their nets were breaking with the weight of all the fish they had caught!

Most nets were edged with weights so they would sink into the water.

Hooks and harpoons were used sometimes. *(Matt. 17:27)*

In addition to cleaning and sorting the fish, fishermen spent a good amount of time mending torn nets. *(Matt. 4:21)*

Fishing boats on the Sea of Galilee were very sturdy. They had oars, probably a central sail, and could hold up to a dozen men.

FULLER

JOB OPPORTUNITY:

The land of Israel is in need of several fullers willing to serve the needs of the Israelites in newly conquered cities.

JOB DESCRIPTION:

We seek qualified fullers with hands-on experience in the art of washing and bleaching wool and cloth. We are an Equal Opportunity Country (EOC) and are interested in men and women alike.

 Sometimes, just the ashes of plants which contained alkali (i.e. soapwort, glasswort and saltwort) were used as "soap."

WE REQUIRE:

All fullers use current, state-of-the-art techniques which include:

• placing newly shorn wool or cloth in large vats of water to be stomped on with experienced feet, or beaten with sticks.

• using only the highest quality soap in the cleansing process. A mixture of alkaline, potash, soda, and herbs is preferred.

• bleaching clean cloth and wool a sparkling white, followed by a thorough rinse in a stream by means of trampling.

OTHER REQUIREMENTS:

• Must be willing to set up shop outside city gates. Fumes from the bleach (which should contain urine and sulfur to be effective) are offensive. Sensitive noses need not apply.

Bible Nugget Malachi 3:2 - The Lord spoke through the prophet Malachi about the coming of Jesus, saying, "He is like a refiner's fire and like fuller's soap." This means that Jesus purifies us and cleanses us.

GATEKEEPER

(ALSO CALLED DOORKEEPER OR PORTER, WATCHMAN)

"WHO GOES THERE?"

At least one gatekeeper was stationed at the gates of a city. He decided who had a right to enter and who didn't. Gatekeepers also guarded public buildings, sheepfolds and temples.

"MORNING IS COMING!"

The watchman stood in the tower at the city entrance or at the gates. He also patrolled the streets. His first job was to keep the people safe from violence. His other job was to call out the hours of the night.

Bible Nugget 2 Sam. 18:24-27 - A watchman looked out from the roof of the city while King David sat between the inner and outer gates. When the watchman saw messengers running toward the city, he called down to the gatekeeper and reported his findings.

12 o'clock!

HERDSMAN

"Rollin', Rollin', Rollin'..."

Herdsmen tended other people's oxen, sheep, goats, or camels. Usually, they were hired by rich owners.

"Though the streams are swollen..."

• They led the animals from oasis to oasis, in search of food and water.

• Whenever possible, they kept the herds in protective folds at night.

• They watched for wild beasts and wandering strays, sometimes from the vantage point of a watchtower.

"Move 'em on, Head em' up..."

Since herdsmen were always on the move, they carried only:

• portable shelter, usually a tent.

• a long cloak which doubled as a blanket.

• a small bag for their provisions - whatever food they could find.

• a sharp goad or pole for prodding the animals.

Bible Nugget Genesis 13:7 - God blessed Abraham and his nephew Lot with so much livestock, they needed many herdsmen to care for them! While traveling to Canaan, Abraham's herdsmen quarreled with Lot's because there was not enough land for all of their cattle to graze.

HUNTER

Hunting began as an honorable means of providing food. Through the years it turned into a sport. Both poor and rich enjoyed hunting, but it was more popular with the wealthy, especially royalty.

How to Hunt

1. Bows and arrows

2. Snares. A device with a cord used to catch quail, partridge, and duck by the leg.

3. Traps. Pits covered with nets and brush used for larger animals like deer, foxes, wolves, bears, lions.

4. Decoys. Cages were filled with birds used to lure an animal in.

5. Falcons. They were trained to strike swift-running gazelle. This enabled a hunter on horseback to catch up to the stunned antelope and trap it in a net.

Bible Nugget Genesis 10:9 - Hunting is one of the oldest occupations of all time. Cush and his son Nimrod were Noah's grandson and great-grandson. Both were mighty hunters!

JUDGE

"All Rise for the honorable Judge Moses..."

When Moses led the Israelites out of Egypt, he was their unofficial judge. He decided what was right and wrong for them. He appointed other judges to help him.

After the Israelites reached Canaan, Joshua divided the land into twelve areas and appointed judges to each one. Judges ruled until Saul became king.

ISRAEL'S JUDGES: Othniel • Ehud • Shamgar • Deborah • Gideon • Tola • Jair • Jephthah • Ibzan • Elon • Abdon • Samson • Eli • Samuel

JUDGE TRIVIA

Judges were the highest leaders of the land and the military commanders.

They were religious leaders by acting as God's spokemen and delivering Israel from her enemies.

They were the administrators of justice.

They were not paid.

They held their office for life and could not appoint their successors.

Their title could not be passed on to their children.

BIBLE HONORS
AND THE AWARD GOES TO . . .

DEBORAH - Most Musical (When she and Barak led the Israelites to victory over the Canaanites, they wrote and sang a song of praise to God!) Judg. 4-5

SAMSON - Most Likely to Succeed (He was called by God to deliver Israel from the Philistines before he was even born!) Judg. 13:6-21

GIDEON - Most Faithful (He trusted God that 300 Israelites could defeat an army of 135,000 Midianites. They did, armed with trumpets, jars, and torches!) Judg. 6-8

EHUD - Most Creative (When Ehud visited the wicked King Eglon to pay the taxes he demanded, he

JUDGE (CONT.)

Much later, judges decided court cases. They didn't even have to know much about law! They held court in the city square, and people would bring their cases to them.

delivered a surprise instead. "I have a message from God for you," he said and pulled out a hidden sword, killing the king.) Judg. 3:12-30

JEPHTHAH - Most Resilient (He was banished by his brothers, called back to help them fight the Ammonites, killed his daughter because of a vow he made to God, then battled with the tribe of Ephraim over a misunderstanding.) Judg. 11; 12:1-7

SAMUEL - Most Dedicated (Before Samuel was born, his mother dedicated him to God's service. He was raised in the tabernacle where Eli taught him to serve God, and he judged Israel for most of his life.) 1 Sam. 1-28

The prophet Samuel was the exception. He traveled from city to city to hold court sessions. *(1 Sam. 7:15)*

Bible Nugget Exodus 18:19-26 - The men Moses chose to serve as judges during the wilderness journey helped set the standard for Israel's future judges. He picked only those who were God-fearing, trustworthy, and honest.

117

MAGICIANS, DIVINERS, SOOTHSAYERS

Magic was an important part of religion in ancient Babylon and Egypt. Those who practiced it claimed to have power which came from other gods or evil spirits.

(ALSO CALLED SORCERERS AND ASTROLOGERS)

MAGIC MISCHIEF

Magicians performed magic. Pharaoh used them to duplicate God's miracles when Moses turned a rod into a serpent, blood into water, and brought frogs upon the land. *(Exod. 7, 8)*

Soothsayers, like the Chaldeans, believed they could tell the future by studying the clouds and stars. King Nebuchadnezzar used them to interpret dreams and

visions. *(Dan. 2:1-4)*

Diviners, like Balaam, foretold future events. Unlike prophets, they were not led by the Spirit of God. *(Num. 22:7)*

Sometimes magicians made up magical formulas which they hoped would bring them money or happiness. They wrote their incantations down on scrolls.

Old Testament Jews were strictly forbidden from practicing magic of any kind by penalty of death. *(Deut. 18:10-19)*

Bible Nugget Acts 19:18,19 - Paul visited the city of Ephesus, a known center of witchcraft and sorcery. While he was there, many of the sorcerers were overcome by the spirit of the Lord, and they publicly burned their magic books.

MERCHANT

Merchants traveled far and wide to find goods which people needed or wanted. In ancient times, they traded their goods door to door. Later, they set up shop in the marketplaces of villages and cities.

→ Travelling merchants stopped at caravansaries located along major trade routes. A caravansary offered shelter, water, and rest during long journeys. Here, the merchants swapped stories and passed on news.

→ Sometimes merchants set up temporary shop at the city gate where people gathered.

→ Shops were crowded side by side. The ones with similar goods were grouped together.

Market Specials

"Attention Shoppers!"

Food and Beverages....

Artichokes and pickled fish - Selected varieties from exotic Spain

Delicate truffles - Jumbo packs; Jerusalem fresh

Meaty plums and figs - Fresh from Palestine and Africa

Dates - Hand-picked from Jericho's date palms

Goat cheese and honey - Large crocks from Sicily

Barley and wheat - By the sack; harvested in Egypt

Oil - Family size.; pressed from flavorful Italian olives

Wine - Delicious vintages of Palestine, Gaul, Greece

Spicy pepper - To flavor and preserve your food! Grown in India.

Other Specials...

Papyrus paper - Made with genuine Nile papyrus

Exotic silks and cottons - Assorted. from China and India

Rugs - All sizes. from Asia Minor

Frankincense and myrrh - Original of Arabia

Cloth - All the way from Britain

Glass - Goblets and bowls hand-blown in Syria

121

MERCHANT (CONT.)

Merchants often used beam balances to weigh their goods. They charged accordingly.

Market inspectors checked the merchant's scales to be sure they were weighted correctly. They also made sure prices were fair. "Crooked" merchants were not uncommon!

Some customers only shopped with merchants who used "king's weights" which were approved by the government.

Most merchants did not own their own ships. They had to borrow money from money lenders to pay for the cost of the cargo and the chartering space aboard the ship.

Bible Nugget Micah 6:11 - The prophet Micah compares Israel to a merchant who uses dishonest scales and false weights. Both will be punished!

MONEY CHANGERS

(ALSO CALLED BANKERS)

Greek, Roman, and Jewish coins circulated throughout Palestine after the Exile. Money changers were needed to exchange money for a different type of currency. They also lent money. Their service was not free. The honest ones charged 5 to 10 percent.

LOAN DEPT.

→ A money changer used a table called a "bank" to conduct his business. He set up shop at marketplaces, harbors, and temples.

MONEY CHANGERS (CONT.)
Exchange Table

CUSTOMER NOTICE!

All Roman taxes must be paid in Roman money!
We will gladly exchange your Greek or Jewish coins.

Don't forget! Have didrachmas on hand to pay the temple tax.

Any shekels in your pocket? You'll need them for temple dues, the poll tax, and redemption from priesthood. Use them to buy lambs and pigeons for sacrifice.

WARNING! Do not attempt to pass false coins! All money is tested and weighed. Criminals will be prosecuted to the fullest extent of Roman law...

Shekels, talents, and pounds were also units of weights in which silver and gold were measured.

 The drachma was officially equal to the denarius, but because it actually contained more silver, it was sometimes accepted more readily than its Roman counterpart!

Israelites were not allowed to charge each other interest, but they could charge interest to Gentiles. *(Exod. 22:25, Deut. 23:20)*

TODAY'S EXCHANGE RATES:

(Currency)	**(Value)**

Roman

quadran: (bronze)	1 quadran = 1 farthing (1/4 cent)
assarion or as: (bronze)	1 assarion = 4 quadrans
denarius: (silver)	1 denarius = 16 assarion

Greek

farthing:	1 farthing = 2 leptons/mites (1/4 cent)
drachma: (silver)	1 drachma = 1 denarius (16 cents)
didrachma: (silver)	1 didrachma = 2 drachmas (32 cents)
tetradrachma or starter: (silver)	1 tetradrachma = 4 drachmas (64 cents)
mina or pound: (silver)	1 mina = 100 drachmas ($16)

Jewish

lepton or mite: (copper)	1 lepton = 1/2 quadran (1/8 cent)
shekel: (silver)	1 shekel = 1 denarius = 1 drachma (16 cents)
talent:	1 talent = 3,000 shekels

MONEY CHANGERS (CONT.)

PRACTICAL VALUE OF ANCIENT MONEY

Bible Nugget Matt. 21:12 - Jesus was angry with the money changers who conducted business in the temple. He overturned their tables and drove them away. Many of them were dishonest and tried to make an unfair profit in the holy temple.

The denarius and the shekel were worth about a day's pay. (Matt. 20:1-16)

One assarion could buy two sparrows. (Matt. 10:29)

Palestinian women received ten drachmas as a wedding gift. (Luke 15:8)

The coin Peter found in the fish's mouth was the tetradrachma. (Matt. 17:27)

Judas was paid thirty tetradrachmas to betray Jesus. (Matt. 26:15)

Thirty shekels was the price of one slave. (Exod. 21:32)

The coins the poor widow gave to the treasury were leptas. (Luke 21:2-4)

MUSICIAN

During the days of Samuel, David, and Solomon, the golden age of Hebrew music was in full swing! Music was very important to the Israelites. Musicians sang or played musical instruments during temple services, special feasts, weddings, and funerals.

Bible Orchestra

STRING:

Harp - Its twelve strings were louder and lower in pitch than the lyre. It was one of the most important instruments in the temple orchestra. (Solomon made harps with imported algumwood - *1 Kings 10:12*. David made them from berosh. Some were decorated with shell, lapis, red limestone, and gold.)

Lyre - Ten strings, made of twisted grass or dried animal intestine, were plucked to make a sweet, soft sound. It was the chief instrument in the temple orchestra. (The lyre, not the harp, was played by young David to soothe King Saul. *1 Sam. 16:23)*

MUSICIAN (CONT.)

Psaltery - It had ten strings and was rectangular-shaped like a zither. It was usually played with the harp and lyre.

Lute - Shaped like a triangular guitar with three strings. (It was played to celebrate the defeat of Goliath by David. *1 Sam. 18:6*)

PERCUSSION:

Bells - Small gold bells or jingles. (High priests, like Aaron, wore them on the hem of their garment. *Exod. 28:33-35*)

Cymbals - Two-handed brass cymbals were loud and large. Smaller, one-handed cymbals had a higher "tinkling" pitch. They were the only permanent percussive instrument in the temple orchestra.

Gong - Used at weddings. Made of brass.

Sistrum or Rattle - Shaken like castanets on joyous occasions. Early sistrums were clay and had small stones inside.

Tambourine - It was beaten like a drum and didn't jingle. Made of two skins stretched over a wooden hoop. (Miriam played it to show her delight in the Lord. *Exod. 15:20*)

called together by the blast of two silver trumpets. *Num. 10:1-3)*

WIND

Organ - This skin-covered box had ten holes through which wind was forced. It made a loud sound.

"WOODWIND"

Oboe - It had two reeds, probably two pipes, and was made of wood, ivory or bone. It made a wailing sound, but was played at joyous celebrations as well as funerals.

Pipe - This was the shepherd's pipe or flute. It was a straight instrument with holes. It was played at celebrations and funerals. (It was one of many instruments used by King Nebuchadnezzar to call the people to worship the golden image. *Dan. 3:5)*

"BRASS"

Shofar - This curved trumpet was made from a hollow ram's horn. It could make only two or three notes, but was very expressive. It was used as a call to worship or battle. (The shofar was played during Joshua's siege of Jericho. *Joshua 6:20)*

Trumpet - It was straight, long, and ended in a bell shape. (In the wilderness, the Israelites were

MUSICIAN (CONT.)

WHICH BIBLE HERO WAS A MIGHTY WARRIOR, A FUTURE KING, AND A GIFTED MUSICIAN?

It was David! He was such a fine musician, he wrote and sang psalms, played the lyre for King Saul, and even invented musical instruments! Later, he appointed four thousand musicians to sing and play in the temple. (1 Chron. 23:5)

Solomon formed a large choir for his temple. It was were led by a choir leader, the musician chief. Solomon provided his musicians with furnished homes and a paid salary.

Solomon also wrote 1,005 songs. *(1 Kings 4:32)*

Bible Nugget 2 Chron. 5:12,13 - When the ark was brought into Solomon's temple, musicians played cymbals, harps, lyres and trumpets. Singers raised their voices to God. The glory of the Lord filled the temple in a thick cloud!

NURSES, MIDWIVES

Nurses acted more like nannies or nursemaids. They were brought into a home to help raise the children and tutor them in their studies. They were respected and often loved like members of the family.

NURSES, MIDWIVES (CONT.)

Midwives helped deliver babies in New Testament times. They would:

1. cut the umbilical cord

2. bathe the infant in water

3. rub the baby down with salt to prevent infection

4. swaddle the baby tightly in long linen strips

 Usually once a day, babies were loosed from their swaddling. They were washed, rubbed with olive oil, and sprinkled with dried myrtle leaves.

* FOR THE FIRST SIX MONTHS, BABIES WERE WRAPPED TIGHTLY TO KEEP THEM FROM THRASHING THEIR ARMS AND LEGS.

Bible Nugget Gen. 24:59, 35:8 - When Rebekah left home to marry Isaac, her nurse went with her. Years later, nurse Deborah died. She was buried beneath an oak tree Rebekah called Allon Bacuth which meant "oak of weeping."

PERFUMER

(ALSO CALLED CONFECTIONER)

Perfume Counter

A perfumer worked to make the finest perfumes, oils, and medicines. In every large village or city, a street of perfumers displayed their wares. These included fragrant powders, pressed cakes, oils, fats, seeds, spices, leaves, and bark.

Nard ($$$$) Rose-red, fragrant ointment. 100 per cent pure. From the roots and stems of the spikenard plant, India.

Balm ($$$$) Perfume oil made from exotic Arabian balm sap and oils.

Frankincense ($$$) Pure teardrop chunks or perfume. From India and Arabia.

Cinnamon Oil ($$$) Sweet cinnamon oil distilled from the cinnamon tree, Sri Lanka (Ceylon).

Cassia ($$) Aromatic bark. Related to cinnamon, but with a less delicate aroma.

Cane or Calamus ($$) Fragrant ointment made from India's ginger-grass.

Eau de Aloe ($$) Perfume made from the fragrant resin of the Eaglewood tree.

Myrrh ($$) A perfume, solid or liquid, made from the scented gum of the Palestine shrub.

Scented Oils ($) A variety of pleasing mixtures using olive oil, fragrant herbs, and flowers like jasmine and rose.

($$$$) 300 or more denarii
($$$) 50 or more denarii
($$) less than 10 denarii
($) less than a denarius

In Jesus' time, a **denarius** = about a day's wages

To Perfume or Not to Perfume?

DO use perfumes and oils:

- to smell sweet *(Esth. 2:12)*
- to cleanse and moisturize the skin *(Ps. 104:15)*
- to protect against sunburn and insect bites
- to anoint an honored guest *(Luke 7:46)*
- for ceremonies and royal coronations *(2 Sam 5:3)*
- for use in the tabernacle or temple *(Exod. 30:26)*
- for preparing a body for burial *(John 19:39)*

CUSTOMER NOTICE!

Each **($$$$)** and **($$$)** purchase comes with its own hand-crafted alabastron to dispense your costly perfume or oils slowly. Hurry! Limited quantity. While supplies last.

PERFUMER (CONT.)

SACRED ANOINTING OIL

500 shekels (12 1/2 lbs.) liquid myrrh
250 shekels (6 1/4 lbs.) fragrant cinnamon
250 shekels of fragrant cane
500 shekels of cassia
a hin (about 4 quarts) of olive oil

Mix together thoroughly. Sacred anointing oil is to be used strictly for holy purposes as ordered by God. Do NOT pour it on men's bodies and do not make any oil or perfume with the same formula. (*Exod. 30:23-24*)

 Kings' perfumers used the blooms of orange trees, violets, and roses to make scented syrup waters. During the summer, guests were served the refreshing beverages in brass tumblers on silver trays!

Bible Nugget Mark 14:3 - Jesus visited the home of Simon the Leper. While he was there, his friend Mary poured an entire jar of costly nard perfume over his head. Others thought she was wasting the pricey perfume, but Mary knew the value of her act!

POTTER

Pottery-making is one of the oldest and most important crafts of all time. Nearly every village had a potter. Potters made storage jars, bowls, plates, cups, basins, cooking pots, decanters, flasks, jugs, lamps, ovens, seals for letters.

ANCIENT POTTERY CLASS

MAKING THE CLAY: Sunday and Monday

1. Dig up some clay-dust from a field or wet clay from a stream bank. *(Matt. 27:7)*

2. Let it weather in the sun for a day or two.

3. Pound out the lumps with your mallet; pick out the twigs and pebbles.

4. Add water and mix it with your feet until smooth. *(Isa. 41:25)*

5. Drain the water off the top. Knead the mixture to remove the air pockets.

(Class Note: For cooking vessels, add sand or crushed stone to temper the clay.)

POTTER (CONT.)

SHAPING THE CLAY: Tuesday morning

1. Shape the clay by hand - free-form. Try making long sausage-like rolls and coiling them up!

2. Or press sheets of clay into wooden molds.

4. Try your hand with a potter's wheel! *(Lam. 4:2)*

5. Let the pieces dry, and trim off any extra material.

DECORATING THE CLAY: Tuesday afternoon

1. Use a knife to chisel decorations into your piece.

2. Brush the container with "slip," a colored cream to fill the pores and smooth the surface.

3. Rub your piece with a stone to make it shiny.

4. You can also try painting on decorations, pressing the clay with a woven rope to achieve an interesting design, or adding pieces of colored clay!

The earliest clay pots were baked in the sun. They were brittle and broke easily. It was later discovered that "firing" pots made them harder and longer lasting.

The first potter's wheels were made of wood and then stone.

FIRING THE CLAY: Wednesday through Friday

1. Make a fire or heat up the kiln! Bake your pieces between 700 and 1,050 degrees celsius for up to three days.

2. You are ready to trade or sell your pottery at the marketplace!

RESTING THE CLAY: Go home! Saturday is the Sabbath

 Jerusalem's painted pottery was fragile and thin. The red ceramic bowls and decanters were luxury items like today's fine china. People felt fortunate if they could afford a complete set.

Bible Nugget Jer. 18:1-6 - The Lord told Jeremiah to go to the potter's house where the prophet saw a potter shaping and reshaping a pot at his wheel. God said he wished Israel was like a piece of clay he could mould in his hands, shaping it until it was just right.

SLAVE

(ALSO CALLED CONFECTIONER)

Slaves were the property of their owners. Many performed hard and unpleasant tasks. They helped build Herod's fortresses by digging, carrying heavy loads, and hauling water. Unlike slaves in recent history, however, they had many rights.

Profile of a Slave

A free citizen who sold himself in exchange for an unpaid debt. (Lev. 25:39)

A poor man who sold himself so his family wouldn't starve.

A thief sold into slavery in exchange for the object he stole. (Exod. 22:3)

A prisoner of war. (Num. 31:9)

A child of a slave. (Exod. 21:4)

Daughters sold by their families as maidservants. (Exod. 21:7)

"DECLARATION OF SLAVE RIGHTS" (in part)

Hebrew slaves:

1. Will not work more than 10 hours a day.

2. Will not work on the Sabbath. *(Exod. 23:12)*

3. Must not be returned to their masters if they flee. *(Deut. 23:15)*

4. May buy their freedom at any time. *(Lev. 25:47-53)*

5. Shall be set free after six years of service - with money and support. *(Deut. 15:12-14)*

6. Shall be set free if they lose an eye or a tooth as a result of being hit by their master. *(Exod. 21:26,27)*

There were Hebrew slaves and non-Hebrew slaves. Hebrew slavery was the mildest form of slavery.

An Israelite could not force another Israelite to be a slave against his will. *(Lev. 25:42)*

SLAVE (CONT.)

Sometimes, slaves chose to not leave their masters after six years of service. An awl was pushed through the slave's ear, marking him as a servant for life. *(Deut. 15:16-17)*

Not all servants were considered slaves.

Slave drivers assigned tasks to slaves and made sure they did their work. Egypt did not have laws to protect slaves so Pharaoh used slave drivers to make the Hebrews' lives miserable. He hoped to crush their spirits so they would lose all hope of ever being set free. *(Exod. 1:11-14)*

A custodian was a male slave who looked after his owner's son until the boy was sixteen years old. He walked him to school and cared for him in other ways.

Bible Nugget Exod. 21:20, 21 - If a master beats his slave with a rod and the slave dies, the owner must be punished. If the slave survives, the owner is not to be punished because the slave is considered his property.

SOLDIER

Through the years, Israelite soldiers faced many powerful foes in war. They won miraculous victories when they were obedient to God and suffered devastating losses due to their sin and rebellion.

ARMY CAMPS
Are you ready to rumble?

"On one side, bearing the name "God's chosen," champions of many miraculous battles, weighing in at hundreds of thousands to over a million, the godly, sometimes haughty.....ISRAELITES. "

"On the other side, bearing a likeness to 'swarms of bees,' champions of deceit, idolatry, and thievery, weighing in at incalculable numbers, begotten of all things rotten......AMALEKITES, AMMONITES, AMORITES, ASSYRIANS, BABYLONIANS, JEBUSITES, MIDIANITES, MOABITES, PHILISTINES."

- In ancient days, every Hebrew over the age of twenty was a soldier. *(Num. 1:3)*
- Each tribe had its own regiment, flag, and leader. *(Num. 2:2,10:4)*

SOLDIER (CONT.)

Marching into Battle

INFANTRY:
Footmen: Nearly all of Israel's early wars were fought with foot soldiers. They carried their weapons and were led into battle by a judge, general, or king. *(1 Sam. 4:10)*

CALVARY:
Horsemen: The Israelites were not permitted to keep large numbers of horses. (Deut. 17:16) Until the time of David, horsemen were not used. *(1 Kings 10:26)*

Charioteers: Egyptian and later Hebrew chariots carried two or three soldiers - a driver, an archer, or spearman, and sometimes a shield-bearer. Assyrian chariots were larger and often held three or four soldiers. *(1 Kings 9:22)*

A force of soldiers was generally divided into two attack divisions:

Division #1:

First Battle Line: spearmen
Second Battle Line: bowmen or archers
Third Battle Line: slingers

Division #2:

These soldiers brought up the rear. They were used as a reserve, and they helped the leader escape in case of defeat.

WHICH TWO SOLDIERS FOUGHT IN THE MOST FAMOUS DUEL IN BIBLE HISTORY?

David and Goliath! For forty days, the Israelites and Philistines camped on either side of a valley, waiting for the other to attack. Finally, Goliath was chosen to represent the Philistines. No Israelite would accept Goliath's challenge to fight until young David bravely stepped forward! *(1 Sam. 17)*

SOLDIER (CONT.)

OFFENSIVE WEAPONS

1. Bows made of wood or reed were as long as five feet! **Arrows** were tipped in metal. Up to thirty arrows were carried in a quiver. • *Arrows were sometimes set on fire and sent from the bow.*

2. Clubs were heavy and spiked. They were used to break armor. In later days, clubs were more like nightsticks.

3. Battle-axes were also called "slaughter weapons." They were used in hand-to-hand combat.

4. Swords had long, broad blades used to cut or thrust. They were usually carried in a sheath on the soldier's left side. • *The Egyptian "khepesh" was a sickle-shaped sword.*

A CALL TO ARMS

An armor-bearer was a personal officer of an army commander. He carried the shield and extra weapons. He was chosen for his bravery and loyalty. Saul, Jonathan, Joab, and Goliath all had one. *(1 Sam. 31:4)*

• The iron shaft of Goliath's spear weighed 15 pounds!

• Soldiers relied upon the public to pay for the equipment and provisions of the army. *(Judges 20:1, 2 Sam. 17:28-29)*

5. Dirk Swords were double-edged and shorter. They were used to slash in hand-to-hand combat. • *Carried by Roman soldiers.*

6. Daggers were mostly used for stabbing in hand-to-hand combat. • *Carried by Roman soldiers.*

7. Spears, Javelins, Lances, Darts were long, thin pieces of wood with stone or metal heads. They were thrown or thrust. • *Javelins used by Roman legionnaires were 6 ft. 9 in. long. The iron tip bended on impact and couldn't be reused by enemies.*

8. Slings, made from a band of leather, were wider in the middle to hold a stone. A soldier held both ends in one hand and swung the sling around his head to gain thrust. When he released one end, the stone flew at its target.

SOLDIER (CONT.)

DEFENSIVE WEAPONS

1. Great Shields were large enough to protect the whole body. Made of woven twigs or leather, they were anointed with oil to preserve them and to allow enemy missiles to glide off them more easily. (Isa. 21:5)

2. Bucklers were small, round shields. They were carried by slingers and archers.

3. Helmets were made of leather, then bronze. Kings' helmets were sometimes gold. Quilted caps were worn beneath to hold the helmets in place. Roman helmets had flaps to further protect the head.

4. Coats of Mail were made of leather and covered with a layer of metal scales. Bronze breastplates, worn under the armor, protected the heart. Kings wore coats of mail with more metal. Roman soldiers wore thick, woolen tunics under their armor.

5. Greaves were metal leg guards.

SOLDIER'S PROVISIONS

wheat and barley flour
roasted grain
beans and lentils
honey and curds
cheese from cow's milk

• Roman soldiers relied upon the emperor, NOT THE PUBLIC, to pay the expenses of the Imperial Army.

• Legionnaires were also trained as combat engineers, surveyors, and architects. They designed and built fortifications, roads, bridges, and aqueducts.

→ ROMAN RANKS

Roman soldiers were elite. They were well-disciplined, organized, paid more, and treated better than any other soldiers at this time.

1. Legion - The common fighting men: heavy infantry, cavalry, archers, light infantry. Special troops operated catapults which shot large arrows, and ballistas which fired stones.

> a. Centurion officer - The most important officer of the legions. Commander of a company of about 100 legionnaires.

2. Auxilia - Non-citizens recruited into the army from conquered or allied countries. "Become a citizen of grand Rome! Join the Auxilia! Serve your new country on the battlefield and become a hero!"

3. The Imperial Guard - Elite soldiers which formed the chief military force in Rome. A small number of these soldiers were chosen to guard the emperor.

> a. Praetorian Guard - Mostly foot soldiers, heavy infantry, archers, lancers, with some cavalry.
> b. Imperial Horse Guard - All cavalry.

5. The Fleet - Sailors and marines served aboard the fleet of the imperial navy. Their main job was to combat piracy and support the other armed services. These soldiers were in the least prestigious branch of the service.

SOLDIER (CONT.)

JOB PERKS

1. Generous pay - especially for the Imperial Guard.

2. Bonuses of up to five years pay for good service.

3. Retirement bonus of 13 to 17 years of pay. Legionnaires retired after 20-25 years; Imperial Guard after 16.

4. Double pay - for soldiers with special duties.

5. Roman citizenship - awarded to Auxilia soldiers after a maximum of 25 years of service.

6. Public praise and rewards - for outstanding service.

• Jews were NOT allowed to join the Roman army.

• A Roman soldier carried his own equipment. In addition to carrying a sword, dagger, and shield (rectangular and stronger now), he toted a 60 pound pack on his back. Heavier supplies were packed on mule carts.

• Roman soldiers pitched leather tents in camps surrounded by a ditch. A stake fence was built on a high embankment of dirt. The general's tent was always in the center.

Bible Nugget Acts 10:1-7 - Cornelius was a centurion in the Italian Regiment stationed in Caesarea. God gave Cornelius a vision and asked him to send for Peter. It was God's plan to have Peter tell this Roman soldier all about Christ!

SPINNER, WEAVER

Spinners turned fibers like wool, flax, or cotton into thread or yarn. Weavers used the thread or yarn to weave cloth and rugs.

Spin It!

1. Wind a bundle of unspun fiber around a stick called a distaff. Hold it in your left hand or put it in your belt.

2. Hold a spindle (a long, tapering rod) in the right hand. Wind the fiber from the distaff onto the spindle twisting as you go.

• The first spindles were made of stone.

• Thread or yarn was dyed different colors - either at home or by the local dyer.

• In Jesus' day, most looms produced cloth only three feet wide. Two pieces of cloth had to be sewn together to make clothing wide enough to fit the average person.

• Weavers also wove "rushes" (hollow-stalked plants) and reeds into baskets.

ANCIENT TEXTILES

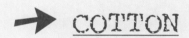 ## COTTON

1. Cotton was imported from Persia into Palestine after the captivity.

2. It was used to make the lining of woolen tunics, long, white underwear, caps, and head scarves.

Weave It!

1. Attach a spool of thread to the shuttle of the loom. Pass it from side to side, moving it over and under vertical threads. Eventually tightly woven cloth is formed.

SPINNER, WEAVER (CONT.)

• Egyptians wove their cotton into a special cloth used to wrap their mummies.

• Wool from the city of Damascus was famous for its whiteness and was eagerly bought at the market. (Ezek. 27:18)

• Egyptian linen was very fine and white and was used to dress Egyptian priests. Pharaoh adorned Joseph in a linen dress. *(Gen. 41:42)*

• Linen was a mark of luxury. *(Luke 16:19)*

 ## <u>WOOL</u>

(a) Wool was one of the first materials used to make cloth.

(b) It was used for tunics, cloaks, girdles (sashes), caps, head scarves, and cords. Israelites were not allowed to wear clothing made of both wool and linen. (Deut. 22:11)

→ <u>LINEN</u>

1. Linen was made from the fiber of the flax plant grown in Egypt and Palestine. It was common to see the plant drying on sunny rooftops. (Josh. 2:6)

2. It was used to make priestly ephods, special tunics, girdles (sashes), turbans, napkins, and lamp wicks. The fabric was strong and kept the wearer cool in the hot desert sun.

Bible Nugget Prov. 31:19, Exod. 35:35 - Wives who practiced the art of spinning were considered to be of noble character. Weavers were thought of as master craftsmen and designers!

TANNER

Tanners made leather from animal hides. While it was a very important trade, tanners were sometimes avoided because their contact with dead animals made them ceremonially "unclean" and unfit to worship God.

How to Prepare a Hide

1. Soak animal skins (usually sheep, goat, badger, ram, jackal, hyena) for several days in a bath of water and old lime.
2. Wash them until the water runs clean.
3. Stretch the skins on a round frame and let dry.
4. Scrape with a sharp knife, removing as many hairs as possible. Rub with pumice, then animal manure.
5. Hammer until soft and flat.

157

TANNER (CONT.)

• Tanners were forced to keep their shops on the outskirts of town, not only because they were "unclean," but also so the wind wouldn't carry offensive odors into the city.

• After animals were sacrificed in the temple, their skins were divided among the priests. They often sold the hides to the town tanners.

• Ram and badger skins were used to cover the tabernacle. *(Exod. 25:5)*

Bible Nugget Acts 9:43 - God gave Cornelius, the Roman centurion, a vision. He was to send for Peter who was staying at the home of Simon the tanner. Even though Simon was considered "unclean," Peter knew he was clean in God's eyes and worthy to spend time with!

TAX COLLECTOR

ALSO CALLED PUBLICAN, TREASURER

Tax collectors collected tax money from the people for the government. Chief tax collectors, like Zacchaeus, worked for the Roman government. Publicans, like Matthew, were ordinary public servants. A treasurer was in charge of all the tax money collected.

• In Roman times, businessmen bid for the right to collect taxes. The highest bidder won. He paid the government an annual fee and kept any additional money he collected.

• Tax collectors were despised because of their habit of overcharging the people and pocketing the difference. Many grew rich this way. Jews disliked them because their money supported the Roman government.

TAX COLLECTOR (CONT.)

ANCIENT TAX FORM (1040 – BIBLE)

TAXES:	PAYABLE TO:	AMOUNT:
Temple tax (Exod. 30:13)	the temple (annually)	half-shekel
Crops, flocks (1 Sam. 8:11-13)	the king	1/10 harvest (also called "obligatory" gifts)
"Building" tax	Solomon - to support his building projects (temple, palaces, etc.)	partly payable in forced labor
Telos tax *(Matt. 17:25)*	Caesar - on goods and travelers (including slaves)	depends on tax man!
Phoros tax	Caesar - on property	1/5 to 1/4 of produce
Kensos tax (also called poll tax)	prince or royal governor for Roman treasury - on persons, houses, lands	denarius

Exemptions:

Priests - you may be exempt because you perform sacred functions. Check with your local officials!

ATTENTION! Pay your taxes on time to avoid costly penalties.

ROYAL DECREE

"All members of the Roman world must return to their hometowns immediately. A census will be taken to count all citizens eligible for taxation or calvary service. Be advised! Those found guilty of withholding information about themselve, their families, or their property will be fully prosecuted."

TAX COLLECTOR (CONT.)

• Heavy public taxes made life very difficult for average citizens. Taxes supported the kings' lavish lifestyles and paid the salaries of public officials, soldiers, and builders.

• Tax collectors set up booths at bridges, city gates, markets, and crossroads. Here, they collected the telos tax on all goods people wanted to sell.

• The title of treasurer belonged to a very important official. Sometimes it was the officer of the state, sometimes the heir to the throne. *(2 Chron. 26:21)*

Bible Nugget Luke 5:27 - Levi, a tax collector, was at his booth when Jesus called to him. Levi left everything to follow him and even held a banquet at his house to honor him. Jesus was criticized for eating with the unrighteous, but he knew these people needed him the most. Levi, later called Matthew, became a great follower of the Lord!

WHAT DID JESUS HAVE TO SAY ABOUT JEWS PAYING TAXES TO THE ROMAN EMPIRE?

Jesus held up a Roman denarius and asked, "Whose image and superscription is this?" When the people replied, "Caesar's," he said, "Render therefore to Caesar the things that are Caesar's; and to God the things that are God's."

TENTMAKER

Tentmakers earned their living making tents from wool, animal skins, or hair. This trade was usually passed down from their fathers. Tents made the perfect house for those who moved a lot, because they could easily take their home with them!

WHO LIVED IN TENTS?

1. **Bible patriarchs like Noah, Abraham, Isaac, Jacob, and Joseph** *(Gen. 9:21)*

2. **Desert nomad tribes like the Bedouins and Nabateans**

3. **The Israelites in the wilderness (Exod. 16:16)**

4. **Soldiers in army encampments and warriors like David** *(2 Kings 7:7;1 Sam. 17:54)*

5. **Workers like carpenters and masons, working on projects away from home**

6. **Herdsmen**

TENTMAKER (CONT.)

• Tentmakers first made tents out of leather. Later, they used goat or camel hair. Goat hair could be woven into a very strong material. It was naturally waterproof and tough enough to stand up under strong desert winds and the scorching sun.

TENT ASSEMBLY INSTRUCTIONS

Model #Goat Hair 101

PARTS LIST	NO. OF PIECES
(a) Woven goat hair	10
(b) Wooden toggles	20
(c) Center wooden pole	1
(d) Wooden perimeter poles	8
(e) ropes	20
(f) stakes	20

To Set Up
(refer to Fig. 1,2,3)

IMPORTANT:
For tech support, contact your local tentmaker!

1. Start assembly with woven goat hair strips (a). Sew them together to form one huge piece.

2. Take wooden toggles (b) and attach them, evenly spaced, around the edges.

3. Pound center wooden pole (c) into the ground.

4. Drive wooden perimeter poles (d) into the ground at desired distance around the center pole.

5. Carefully spread the goat hair covering over the poles.

6. Tie ropes (e) to the toggles. Pound stakes (f) into the ground. Securely attach each rope to a stake.

TENTMAKER (CONT.)

TENT TALK

1. Wooden poles were as high as 7 ft. with the tallest pole in the center. While the average family had nine poles, important families always had more.

2. Tents were made to order - round, tapered, flat, or oblong.

3. Rich families and sheiks had several tents. There were separate tents for women, children, and servants. The main tent was in the center.

4. Tent doors were kept open to welcome visitors.

5. When tents were worn or torn, they were patched with pieces of skin or woven hair.

6. The very best goats' hair, called cilicium, came from the Roman province of Cilicia. Paul learned the art of tentmaking in his hometown of Tarsus in Cilicia!

• The tabernacle in the wilderness was a tent sanctuary. *(Exod. 26:7)*

Bible Nugget Acts 18:3 - When Paul traveled during his missionary journeys, he was able to make money by working as a tentmaker - a trade he learned as a boy. On the Sabbath, he taught in the synagogue and on the other days he made tents!

OTHER OCCUPATIONS

→ **Butchers** in New Testament times set up shop in a part of town called the Street of Butchers. Customers were wealthy because the poor could not afford fresh meat.

→ A **cook** in early times was the mistress of the house. Later, professional cooks were used.

→ A **counselor** was a chief man in government who advised the king on important matters. In Jesus' day, he was a member of the Sanhedrin.

→ **Innkeepers** did not have good reputations in Roman times. They were supposed to take care of travelers' needs, but their inns were often noisy, dirty, and full of bugs.

→ **Professional mourners** were called in by a family to express public grief at a funeral. The more money a family had, the more mourners it could afford to hire.

→ **A post** was a courier or runner. He delivered messages or letters speedily, first by foot and later by horseback. A post was often employed by a king.

➡ **Schoolmasters** supervised the education of scholars and taught them manners. They were known to be very strict

➡ **Sergeants** were Roman officers known as "rod holders." They inflicted the punishment sentenced upon prisoners or lawbreakers.

➡ **Tetrarchs** were the rulers of provinces in the Roman empire. The title of king was often bestowed upon them.

LAND TRAVEL, TRADE

SEE **M**ERCHANT

"BIBLE-BEST" RATES GROUND TRANSPORT

MPD = miles per day
SC = stowage capacity
DF = durability factor
O = options

4 staffs = superior
3 staffs = excellent
2 staffs = average
1 staff = poor

Camel (4 staffs)

MPD: 25 to 30
SC: 400 lbs. of goods and traveler
DF: Could survive more than two weeks without water, walk through wind storms and on blistering sand.
O: Used for solo travel or in caravans moving goods along trade routes.

Carriage   (3 staffs)

MPD: 25 to 45

SC: Large, covered carriages had room for more goods or travelers.

DF: Heavy wagons were used on rough roads, but they had to be driven slowly because the ride was bumpy.

O: Used by couriers or private travelers. Could be "hired" at the town gates in two sizes: light, two-wheeled carts or heavy, four-wheeled wagons.

Mule/Donkey   (3 staffs)

MPD: 20 miles or more

SC: Can carry and pull heavy loads.

DF: Quick, sure-footed on mountain terrain, could endure long journeys.

O: Used for personal travel or to carry goods across trade routes.

Foot (2 staffs)

MPD: 15 to 20

SC: Whatever could be carried.

DF: Depended on age, health of traveler.

O: Traveled on rough or smooth terrain.

Horse   (1 staff)

MPD: 25 to 30

SC: Average load.

DF: few traveled with horses. Stirrups were unknown: saddles were mere blankets.

O: None. Horses were rarely used for travel. They were too expensive and uncomfortable.

LAND TRAVEL, TRADE (CONT.)

Litter (1 staff)

MPD: few
SC: Little to none.
DF: Designed to be luxurious, not durable.
O: Rider rode on a covered, curtained couch, balanced on the shoulders of six or eight slaves or a pair of mules harnessed to the carrying poles. Only for the wealthy.

• The average person traveled by foot or donkey. The poor could never afford a carriage or a camel. *(Acts 19:1;1 Sam. 25:18)*

Early Roads

At first, roads were just paths worn down by travelers. They were not smooth, but filled with rocks, weeds, and thorny bushes. *(Isa. 62:10)*

ROMAN ROADS

1. They were built for the Roman army for swift transport of their soldiers and messengers, but they were used by private citizens, too.

2. The most important highways were paved with huge stones, 18 inches across, 8 inches thick.

3. Roads were very straight, up to 12 feet wide, and sloped for drainage.

4. Milestones marked the distances to cities.

• Travelling was risky business, especially for those who went by foot. Highway thieves hid along the roads and waited for the opportunity to ambush travelers. *(Judg. 9:25)*

CARAVANS

Men and camels formed caravans to transport goods along land trade routes. Each group was organized by a caravan commander. They traveled in a series of relays along endless stretches of desert, one caravan relieving the other at certain points.

Some Caravan Imports

a. frankincense, myrrh - from Arabia
b. fine rugs, embroideries - from Asia Minor
c. spices, drugs, ivory, cotton, silks -
    from India, China, Africa
d. bitumen (petroleum tar)
    - from Mesopotamia

LAND TRAVEL, TRADE (CONT.)

• Some goods from faraway countries first had to be shipped to distant ports. From these ports, they were loaded onto caravans where they were carried along the inland trade routes.

"BIBLE-BEST" REVIEWS INNS – THE BEST AND THE WORST

ABEL'S OASIS (Thumbs up!)

This roadside inn is a jewel in the desert. Located outside palm-studded Jericho, Abel's Oasis offers weary travelers many amenities: clean sleeping rooms (we didn't spot one bedbug), a roomy courtyard for vehicles, animal stables, and a well to refresh. The perimeter gate, locked tight at night, made us feel like we were sleeping in a fortress!

Sleeping mats, oil lamps, chamber pots (toilets) free of charge! The standard BYOF (bring your own food) policy does apply here. Come prepared. Our headdress off to Abel's Oasis! You've won the **GOLDEN DREAM AWARD** for excellence in service!

CAIN'S COURTYARD (Thumbs down!)

Located in the heart of Joppa, Cain's Courtyard is a dreary example of how NOT to run an inn. One stinky latrine was tucked in a corner so remote, I wandered an hour before I located it. (I was sorry when I did.) I bedded down for the night with bedbugs most ungracious, and lay awake on a sliver of mat listening to cartwheels creaking and sailors cursing.

I am exhausted and irritable from my very brief visit to Cain's Courtyard. For that reason, I am pleased to present this so-called-inn with the **ROTTEN NIGHTMARE AWARD** for horrendous service.

- Most inns were like Cain's Courtyard! Travelers tried to stay with friends. Government officials and other important people stayed at the homes of mayors or magistrates.

LAND TRAVEL, TRADE (CONT.)

HOW DID TRAVELERS COMMUNICATE WITH THEIR LOVED ONES BACK HOME?

The wealthy had personal couriers. Most, however, hoped to find someone traveling in the right direction willing to deliver their mail. A letter was written on one side of a sheet of paper and rolled up or folded. A simple address might read, "To Mary from your husband Joseph." It was tied, then sealed with a piece of wax impressed with their private seal.

Bible Nugget Exod. 2:20 - Inns were not necessary in very ancient days. People lived by the "rule of hospitality." Travelers were invited into homes where they were fed, refreshed, and given a place to sleep, if necessary.

SEA TRAVEL, TRADE

SEE **S**AILOR

The Israelites spent most of their time on land, rather than sea. Their neighbors, the Philistines and the Phoenicians, as well as the Greeks and Romans, designed and built many of the ships which sailed the Mediterranean and beyond.

COMMON SAILING SHIPS

1. Great Merchant Ships (Large vessels with two oversized oars for rudders, a tiller, a square mainsail, and sometimes more sails.)

   A. Alexandria to Rome Freighters
   Each could carry 1,300 tons of grain from Egypt to Rome. (Acts 27:6)

   B. Greek and Roman Freighters
   Carried 70 to 400 tons of goods, depending on size. Traded up and

SEA TRAVEL, TRADE (CONT.)

down the Mediterranean coast, south to Egypt, north to Asia Minor.

C. Ships of Tarshish
King Solomon's fleet of Phoenician ships sailed by expert Phoenician sailors. Traded to Spain, Ophir, and southern India. *(1 Kings 9-10)*

2. Merchant Galley (Swift, slender vessels, powered and steered by a bank of oars pulled by crews. Usually had a square sail.)

A. Phoenician Trireme
Invented by the Phoenicians, it had three banks of oars. Sailed it to Cornwall for tin and to the Canary Islands.

B. Small Galleys
Used to carry cargo and people for short hauls along the coasts or between the islands. Some weren't much bigger than rowboats.

• Passenger vessels did not exist. Travelers walked up and down the waterfront waiting for a cargo ship that was going in their direction and was willing to take them aboard. They had to take along enough food to last the entire trip. *(Acts 27:6)*

• In ancient days, captains consulted their passengers before they made major decisions about their voyage. A majority vote ruled. *(Acts 27:9-12)*

• Grain was easily carried in sacks or bins.

• Wine and olive oil were poured into tall, clay jars called amphorae. Resin was smeared on the inside so the liquid wouldn't seep out. The cork was sealed with clay or cement. Their pointed bottoms allowed them to sink deep into sand to stay cool.

Main Overseas Imports
(shipped out of Palestine or surrounding areas)

a. grain – Egypt
b. wine – Italy, later France
c. olive oil – Italy, later Spain

Main Overseas Exports
(shipped out of Palestine or surrounding areas)

a. glassware – Syria
b. balsam – Palestine
c. cedar – Lebanon
d. purple dye – Tyre

SAILORS' SUPERSTITIONS

Sailors were very superstitious. Voyages were delayed or cancelled because of dreams or omens which they believed had mystical meaning.

SEA TRAVEL, TRADE (CONT.)

Dreams of . . .

1. Turbulent waters or anchors - meant a voyage must be delayed
2. Goats - meant big waves and a storm
3. Black goats - meant big waves
4. Bulls goring someone - meant shipwreck
5. Owls - meant storm, pirate attack

Bad Omens . . .

1. Someone who sneezes while walking up the gangplank.
2. A glimpse of wreckage on shore.
3. A crow or magpie croaking in the rigging before the ship departed.
4. Clipping one's nails during good weather.
5. Dancing on board.
6. Death aboard a ship - the worst omen of all.

Good Omens:

1. Dreams of flying on one's back or walking on water.
2. Birds sitting in the rigging during a voyage meant land was near.

• Ancient lighthouses were used only to mark harbor entrances. They did not warn of rocky areas or impending storms.

WHAT WAS THE BIGGEST THREAT TO ANCIENT SHIPS BESIDES SHIPWRECK?

It was the marine borer, a wormy creature that tunnels into submerged wood. Sailors nailed thin sheets of lead to the outside of the hull to keep out the destructive pest!

Bible Nugget Acts 27-28 - During Paul's voyage to Rome aboard an Alexandrian grain ship, he faced turbulent waters and hurricane-strength winds. The ship was tossed about for 14 days before it finally crashed off the coast of Malta. God spared the lives of all 276 passengers.

BATTLE READY

SEE SOLDIER

SPECIAL NEWS REPORT

On the scene at Gilgal.....

"I'm standing in the camp at Gilgal where Joshua, commander of the Israelites, just returned from a victorious battle at Gibeon. His men are weary, but jubilant.

Yesterday, Gibeon was attacked by an alliance of Amorite kings and begged for Israel's help. Joshua received this word from the Lord, "Do not be afraid of them. I have given them into your hand..."

BATTLE TIPS

(2 Sam. 19-25)

1. Ask God if you should fight. (Pray, seek God through a prophet, or see a high priest who will consult the Urim and Thummim.)

2. Follow God's instructions carefully.

3. Give God the glory.

Israel marched all night to wage a surprise attack. After successfully driving the Amorites from Gibeon, the Israelites chased them through the Valley of Aijalon. One eyewitness said, "The Lord tossed huge hailstones down, and the Amorites dropped like flies. The sun stood still, and Joshua finished them off."

Yet another victory for a brilliant strategist. Back to you...." *(Josh. 10:1-15)*

WHAT WERE THE URIM AND THUMMIM?

The Urim and Thummim were precious stones or small, flat objects used only by the high priest. The priest prayed to God for guidance, asked a simple "yes" or "no" question, and shook out the stones. Each stone had a "yes" and "no" side. If both stones were "yes," the answer was "yes." If both were "no," the answer was "no." One "yes" and one "no" meant "no reply." *(Lev. 8:8; 1 Sam. 14:37-42)*

BATTLE READY (CONT.)

Battle Protocol

1. Blow a trumpet to announce the opening and closing of each battle. *(2 Sam. 2:28)*

2. Take the ark to ensure God's help and a priest to find God's will. *(Judg. 6:36)*

3. Priests - address the army: "Hear O Israel, today you are going into battle against your enemies. Don't be fainthearted or afraid; do not be terrified or give way to panic before them. For the Lord your God is the one who goes with you to fight for you against your enemies to give you victory." *(Deut. 20:2-4)*

4. Army officers - address the army: "Is any man afraid or fainthearted? Let him go home so that his brothers will not become disheartened too." *(Deut. 20:9)*

5. Army officers appoint the commanders. *(Deut. 20:9)*

6. Offer up a sacrifice. *(1 Sam. 7:8-10)*

7. Make an offer of peace before attacking a city. If they don't accept, **LAY SIEGE!** *(Deut. 20:10-12)*

BATTLE READY (CONT.)

BATTLE STRATEGIES

AMBUSH - army lies in wait, then attacks by surprise. *(Josh. 8:3)*

FEINT - a mock attack in one area to distract attention from the real point of attack. *(Judg. 20:20)*

FLANK ATTACK - an army attacks the side (flank) of a body of troops where it is weaker. *(2 Sam. 5:22)*

SURPRISE ATTACK - a sneak attack intended to catch the enemy off guard and unprepared. *(Josh. 11:1-2)*

RAID - a surprise, hostile attack by a smaller force of men. *(1 Chron. 14:9)*

FORAY - a raid, often for the purpose of taking enemy spoils or loot. *(2 Sam. 3:22)*

FORAGING FOR SUPPLIES - a raid for the purpose of taking needed provisions - usually food. *(2 Sam. 23:11)*

BATTLE READY (CONT.)

• Booty, plunder, spoils, loot - all names for goods taken from the enemy in battle. Booty was divided equally between those who went into battle and those who stayed behind. Parts were given to the Lord, the Levites, and the king. *(Num. 31:27-30; 2 Kings 14:14)*

SIEGE TACTICS

The Attacker: Build up tall mounds of earth around the city walls. Carry or roll your battering ram (large wooden beam with a metal ram's head attached) to the top of the mound. Use it to break holes in the city walls.

The Attacked: Try to drive off the enemy. Shoot arrows from the walls, throw darts and stones.

• Battering rams were first carried on the shoulders of men. Later, they were mounted on frames or rollers. Some were covered with armored roofs to protect the soldiers from arrows and spears. A few ancient rams weighed 150,000 pounds and needed 1,000 men to operate them!

• The Roman balista shot stones, while the catapult shot large arrows.

• Most fortified cities were surrounded by moats and one or two walls topped with walkways and towers. Ancient Jerusalem had three walls with 164 towers or parapets!

TRUE OR FALSE

Test your ancient battle know-how:

1. When horses were trained for war, they wore bells around their necks to help them get used to noise.

2. When Israel captured a city, the people in it were always killed.

3. Sometimes, prisoners of war were blinded by their enemies.

4. Conquerors put their feet on the necks of their captives as a sign that they were victorious over their enemies.

5. All trees in besieged cities were torched and burned by the Israelites.

1. True. *(Zech. 14:20)* **2. False.** God allowed for the women and children in certain cities to be taken as plunder and sold as slaves. *(Deut. 20:14)* **3. True**. Their eyes were sometimes gouged out as an act of particular cruelty. *(Judg. 16:21)* **4. True** *(Josh. 10:24)* **5. False.** Fruit trees were saved, the fruit eaten. The wood of other trees was used to make siege works, like battering rams. *(Deut. 20:19-20)*

Bible Nugget Judges 7:16 - Sometimes, battles were waged at night. Gideon led the Israelites to the Midianite camp at about 10 p.m. God told him to take three hundred men, trumpets, and empty jars with torches inside! He was victorious.